HOME
HARMONY

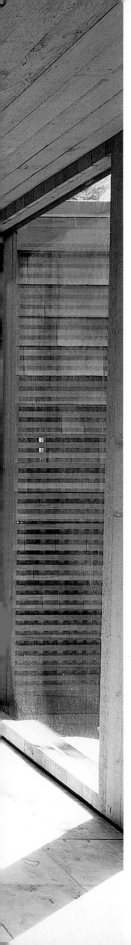

HOME
HARMONY

SUZY CHIAZZARI

**Using the five elements to
create a blissful, balanced home**

Trafalgar Square Publishing

First published in the United States of America in 2001 by
Trafalgar Square Publishing, North Pomfret, Vermont 05053

Colour separated in Milan by Colorlito S.r.l.

Printed and bound in Singapore by Tien Wah Press

1 3 5 7 9 10 8 6 4 2

Editor: Nicky Thompson
Designer: Christine Wood
Picture researcher: Claire Gouldstone

ISBN 1-57076-174-4

Library of Congress Catalog Card Number: 00-104936

The papers used are natural, recyclable products made from wood
grown in sustainable forests.

CONTENTS

Foreword 6

The five elements 8

Landscape 28

WOOD 50

FIRE 62

EARTH 74

METAL 88

WATER 100

Honoring the five elements 112

Useful addresses 124

Further reading/Acknowledgments 126

Index 127

FOREWORD

In the 1970s James Lovelock developed the theory of Gaia. This visionary concept, which took its name from the Greek earth goddess, proposed that the earth is a super organism hurtling through space. Lovelock's theory was that living organisms, including ourselves, do not merely adapt to conditions on earth, but that we interact with our surroundings in order to maintain a mutually beneficial environment. He saw the planet as one collective entity or self-regulating system.

This seemingly radical idea, that the planet is actually alive, is rapidly gaining acceptance by environmentalists and some scientists. Although some people view this concept as entirely new, many philosophies embrace the inter-connectedness between all living things, including the earth. For me, the most striking of these originates in China and is embodied in the ancient Taoist beliefs.

Tao is the thread linking human beings to their surroundings, firstly with their homes and gardens and secondly with nature and the cosmos. The Taoist monks observed that on this physical plane, the basic life force or Chi manifests in several forms or elements. These include minerals, fluids, gases, and the electro-magnetic forces of light, wind, and sound. They identified these forces on earth in the five basic elements of metal, earth, wood, water, and fire.

The ways in which the elements relate to one another were used as a means to understanding life, for man and nature are governed by the same laws. The Chinese believed that if we could change and balance our surroundings we could also balance and improve our own lives. Today we can use the model of the five elements to give us an insight into the way in which this self-regulating system works and how it affects our lives.

Just as modern scientists confirm that we share the same atomic make-up as our planet, the Taoists believed that everything on earth consists of one or a combination of the elements, and that the human organism embodies differing combinations of all five. Our physical bodies are made up of water, earth, and minerals, while we take in the wood element through our food. All our metabolic and body systems are dependent on light, and at a spiritual level, the element of fire represents the divine spark within us. So whether you take a scientific or a philosophical view of life, our good health depends on the harmonious interchange of energy between the five elements within the different parts of our being.

While the five elements are present in our physical bodies, each element also has certain qualities with which we have an intuitive affinity. Our predisposition towards an element reflects our personality type, emotional and mental state. We naturally feel more comfortable in an environment which reflects our individual elemental make-up and at the same time these elements in our surroundings make us feel relaxed and at home.

It is the interplay of the five elements which shapes our environment, which is as alive as we are. Rather than merely adapting to our environment we have to interact and cooperate with it. Our relationship with the environment creates and maintains stability within our own system and that on earth.

In this book, I will show you how to identify the predominant forces flowing in and around you, so that you can create a home full of health and vitality. Understanding the relationships between the different elements is not only a means of self-knowledge but allows you to work with, and not against, the natural systems. By going with this flow you can create a stable and healthy environment within you and in your immediate environment.

When we go through times of stress, we instinctively seek out nature. Wood and water create a harmonious mix which relaxes and

soothes our nerves. By bringing these two elements indoors we can draw on the healing qualities of these elements. Sometimes specific elemental energy can enhance the quality of our lives. When we are restless and disorganized, it is the simple strength and focus of metal that comes to our aid and when we are feeling tired or depressed the fire element can cheer us up. By sympathetically adjusting the five elements in your home, you can interact with your environment in a positive and nurturing way. In return, your home will give you support and nourishment especially during difficult times so that you can enjoy a peaceful and harmonious life.

THE FIVE
ELEMENTS

INTRODUCTION

We once lived most of our lives out of doors, exposed to the elements. We awoke at sunrise and went to sleep when darkness fell. We understood the movements of the sun and the planets and our lives were based around the daily and seasonal rhythms in nature.

All that has changed, and today most people spend over 80 percent of their time indoors. Compared with our ancestors, we certainly have improved living conditions in that we can build excellent shelters which protect us from the extremes of cold and heat, and we have harnessed water and other natural resources to make our lives more comfortable. While this artificially created environment has eased our physical needs, it has not been so beneficial for our emotional and spiritual welfare. The more we distance ourselves from nature and natural rhythms the more stressed we become.

I believe that we urgently need to redress this balance, and come to a closer understanding of nature since our alienation from the natural world is the root cause of many of our ills. A number of people are already trying to lead a more balanced and natural life, spending time, energy, and money on healthy eating, and exercising their body and mind. This is an excellent start, but unless these principles are extended to the environment, all the good that is being done may be undermined.

In order to live a healthy and balanced life we need to preserve and create conditions in which we can flourish and grow. One of the most effective ways to do this is by creating a home which connects to the natural flow of energy, or Chi, pervading the landscape. In the Taoist art of feng shui, which literally means "wind and water", buildings and objects are intentionally arranged to encourage the flow of Chi through our homes. By using feng shui in a modern context, we can link ourselves to our immediate environment, and this connection will have positive benefits in all areas of our lives.

For hundreds of years we have plundered the earth, and it is essential that we now give something back to the earth, if we are to maintain any quality of life. The planet on which we live is a complete and self-sustaining system and our own bodies mirror this order in miniature. Whatever happens around us will also affect our lives and so we need to harmonize the relationship between our external and internal environments. It is through our home, which can be described as our third skin, that we are able to connect and communicate with natural phenomena and once again play our part in the web of life.

Theories of the five elements

Our perception of the world influences how we live. Our beliefs are turned into thoughts and we make sense of our world and ourselves accordingly. How we view life has a profound effect on our behavior and lifestyle.

Throughout history different cultures have held the belief that all life occurs within the circle of nature, and that this is a coherent and unified system. Everything in nature is connected and mutually dependent. All matter, from rocks and plants to living creatures, is composed of mutual "building blocks" of energy. The form this energy takes mirrors the basic structure and patterns of the universe.

Central to philosophies from all over the world is the idea of wholeness being brought about by bringing together different elements into a unified system. The four elements were thought of as the primary constituents in the universe. In Western tradition, influenced mainly by Greek philosophy, these were the elements of earth, air, fire, and water to which a fifth, ether, was added. Ether can be viewed as the quintessential spirit which enlivens the other elements. It was the Greek philosopher Empedocles (c. 450 BC), who first classified the fundamental four elements. Later, Plato (c. 428–348 BC) viewed the four elements as the basic building blocks of life and ascribed to them geometric shapes and mathematical numbers. His pupil, Aristotle (384–322 BC) carried this idea further. He proposed that primary matter first existed as pure potentiality and later actualized into a reality.

During medieval times, the alchemists reverted to a more simplistic idea, that the world originated from a single substance which separated in to the four elements of earth, air, fire, and water. These elements combined into various proportions to make up all the objects of the world. They believed that it was possible to change all matter into gold if they could find the secret to manipulating the elements of other substances.

In the East, the five-fold Indian symbolic system of the five elements was based on the belief of cosmic "states of vibration." This idea was set out in the *Samkhya-karujas* written by Ishvarakrsna, in the 3rd century AD. The five elements defined by him were *akasha* (ether), *apas* (water), *vayu* (air), *tejas* (fire), and *prithivi* (earth).

Because the elements were viewed as the basis of cosmic order and harmony, early medicine sought to balance the physical and temperamental characteristics assigned to each. The Ayurvedic system, which developed many thousands of years ago in India, associates the four qualities of hot, cold, wet, and dry to the archetype forces active within us. Today, branches of complementary medicine based on these principles still give the connection between order and balance great importance. The four elements were not only seen as pervading the physical body but also the mind. The Swiss psychologist Carl

Jung (1875–1961) used the four elements to represent distinct types of human characteristics: intuition (fire), thinking (air), feeling (water), and sensation (earth). Psychologically, we are all made up of a combination of these.

Perhaps the best-known system relating to the five elements is that based on the Taoist system which developed in China. In mystical terms, the elements are the basis of, as well as the life-giving force behind, the material universe.

The Chinese call this life-nurturing energy in its undifferentiated state the Tao. In Western thought, this is the creative soup out of which everything is formed. It is often referred to as cosmic consciousness or universal mind, while religions think of this life-giving force as the "divine" or "God." The Chinese thought of the Tao as holding the potential for all things so that everything is possible and at soul level we are part of the Tao.

WHEN WOOD, FIRE, EARTH, METAL, AND WATER ARE PRESENT THEY BALANCE EACH OTHER TO CREATE PERFECT HARMONY.

The five elements correspond to the seasons and the quality of energy during the yearly cycle:

■ Wood represents expansion and is linked to spring.

■ Fire represents completion and is linked to summer.

■ Earth represents transition and is linked to late summer.

■ Metal represents contraction and is linked to autumn.

■ Water represents consolation and is linked to winter.

There are no specific proportions of yin and yang in the different elements because elemental energy is in a constant state of flux. For example, rocks have more yang than sand although both embody the earth element. Generally, however, when the elements are compared:

■ Fire is the most yang element.

■ Water is the most yin element.

■ Wood has more yang than yin.

■ Metal has more yin than yang.

■ Earth contains about the same amount of yin and yang.

The duality of life

Tao is manifest in all things through the dynamic interaction of the two polar energy forces, yin and yang. There is yin and yang in everything in the universe and there is no absolute yin or absolute yang. They coexist with each other in the same way that good is balanced by evil, and darkness is linked to light. The yin/yang sign is always shown with a small dot of the opposite color in the middle of the yin/yang symbols, as a reminder that order and harmony are maintained by an interplay of these cosmic forces.

Using this model of life, good health can be viewed as a state of energy balance. The dynamic force of yin and yang energy is constantly circulating within the body and is a necessary condition of life. In order to secure good health, we are striving to create a balance in our lives and bodies through an interplay of these two opposing forces.

Yin and yang manifest in varying proportions in all things, so some things are more yin while others are more yang. Yin and yang energy each have their own qualities. Yin energy is the feminine force which is receptive and inactive, while yang is the masculine force and relates to giving and communicating.

The Tao therefore is based on an interplay between the masculine and feminine polarities that exist at a subtle and unseen level. According to Chinese philosophy, at the physical (as opposed to the spiritual) level, the Tao manifests in five basic elements that interact in a creative cycle to form all other substances. These elements are fire, water, earth, metal, and wood and they possess varying proportions of yin and yang energy. Fire is the most yang, while water is the most yin. The other three elements fall in the middle, with differing amounts of yin and yang.

When there is a balance between the five elements within us and within our immediate environment, we are blessed with a happy, healthy, and fulfilling life.

How the elements interact with one another

The ancients were not so naive as to believe that the literal basis of matter is comprised of the five elements, although nature is curiously suggestive of this. Matter does tend to present itself in four guises, as solids (metal and earth), liquids (water), gases and electro-magnetic phenomena (fire). Wood is a combination of earth and water. Each substance has its own special qualities and influence on its neighbors.

By looking at the physical universe holistically, each element can be identified with a planet, season, color, and compass direction. As our system mirrors the external universe, the elements can be linked to our body organs and systems, to our senses, and to our emotions.

In the Tao philosophy, the five elements interact with one another in two distinct ways. Firstly they interact in a creative way, with each element fueling and supporting the next and secondly, they interact in a destructive way, where each element destroys the next.

In the creative cycle the color of each element gives support to the color of the next one, while in the destructive cycle the colors negate and control the effects of the following element. The colors linked to the elements are:

FIRE   RED
WOOD   GREEN
EARTH   YELLOW
WATER   BLUE/BLACK
METAL   WHITE

If you live in a house where the elements are in conflict with your own elemental make-up, you will be setting the destructive process in motion. So by understanding the relationships between the elements and the different effects they have on each other, you can enhance and promote the qualities of the constructive cycles in your own body and life.

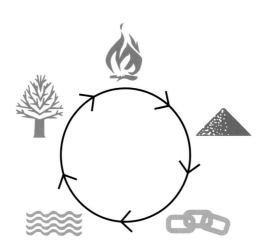

THE CREATIVE CYCLE IS INDICATED BY THE ARROWS.

In the creative cycle, fire creates earth by forming ashes, and earth creates metal because metal is formed within the earth. Metal creates water through the process of condensation, and water creates wood by feeding plant life. Wood in its turn acts as a fuel for fire.

THE DESTRUCTIVE CYCLE IS INDICATED BY THE DOTTED LINE.

In the destructive cycle, fire destroys metal by melting it, metal destroys wood by chopping it, wood destroys earth by covering it, earth destroys water by damming it and water destroys fire by washing it out.

The five elements in our lives

The human organism is a self-regulating system, and a microcosm of nature. We cannot separate ourselves from nature, because we are an inextricable part of it. What happens in the natural world will ultimately affect us, and *vice versa*.

Unfortunately, modern Western thought has changed our set of beliefs to make us think that we are separate from nature. This is reflected in our modern lifestyle, where we spend most of our lives indoors away from natural light and elements.

While we forge ahead with advances in science and manufacturing in the belief that it is of benefit to humanity as a whole, at the same time we are also losing valuable knowledge and understanding of our environment and indeed our own nature. Although the human brain has evolved at speed, we are trapped within bodies that are slow to change and that are still regulated by the same systems as they were thousands of years ago.

The fine balance between giving ourselves a modern and safe living environment while maintaining our connection with nature has been lost. The result is reflected in many new illnesses and diseases which never occurred previously. Not only is our physical health suffering but our mental health. Stress is on the increase and our emotional relationships are also under pressure.

It would be extremely difficult to change our lifestyles completely and to live closely with nature once again, so we need to look for an alternative, more practical solution. Our homes provide us with the perfect tool for renewing this link and influencing our moods, well-being, and happiness.

Symbolic representations of the five elements around the home remind us that everything we do affects and is affected by the natural environment. By using building materials and objects made from earth, wood, and metal, and by creative use of water and fire, we are able to interact more directly with the elemental energy they carry. This helps us establish a positive relationship with nature which directly affects our own quality of life.

The benefits of using the five elements in your home

The home is a living, breathing thing. Whatever its style, it is fashioned from materials and elements found on our planet. It is an extension of the natural environment. We relate to our homes in a very intimate and personal way, and through this relationship we can also connect to the outside world. Our homes not only provide us with shelter and protection from hostile and stressful forces, they also allow us to reach out to others and the world about us without fear of harm.

The elemental qualities contained and represented in your home can have a marked effect on your quality of life. To thrive, you need to relate to your home as a friend and like a friend, your home needs to have sympathetic and understanding qualities. Through its energy systems, your home will provide you with a nourishing and supportive environment.

Most people would not dream of hanging around someone who got on their nerves and was always pulling them down and yet we are often willing to live in spaces which do exactly the same thing. Living in a home which is out of balance creates negative energy patterns which eat their way into our own systems.

The planet on which we live is a complete self-sustaining system and our own body mirrors this order, in miniature. In order to lead a healthy and happy life we need to harmonize the relationship between our external and internal environments. These two ecosystems do not exist separately and it is through a third ecosystem, that of the house, that we are able to connect and communicate with natural phenomena.

When we build our homes we already utilize the natural alchemy of the materials themselves. Glass is made through the interaction and exchange of energy between sand, soda, and limestone, while metal structures are made as a result of interaction between different minerals. In the manufacture of many of these materials, it is the element of fire which enables these wonderful changes to occur. Fire has powerful transformative qualities, and can be brought into our lives when we need to instigate change.

By inviting the forces of nature into your home you will be creating a miniature universe to which you can easily respond. There are many ways to introduce the five elements, in a subtle and symbolic way. In the simplest form, the elements have physical substance, and you can find them in the building materials, furnishings, and objects around your home. On another level, each element creates an atmosphere or feeling, which affects the more subtle parts of our being.

Sensual deprivation

Perhaps the most fundamental reason for having a balance of the five elements in your home is that it can provide you with a good opportunity to live a stimulating and fulfilled life.

The human child needs many years of nurturing and teaching to achieve its full potential and development. One of the basic requirements for our physical and emotional growth is loving touch, without which we grow up finding it hard to form loving relationships and to respect and celebrate our own bodies.

The ability to enjoy touch and tactile stimulation starts at an early age, when babies need to explore and experience the world with all their senses. As well as looking and touching, infants have a natural curiosity and always try to test and discover more about objects by putting them in their mouths. Similarly, food is not just there to be tasted, but needs to be felt with the hands. Although adults may try to prevent this behavior, oral experimentation is a perfectly natural and essential part of growing up.

THE CORNER OF THIS ROOM STIMULATES ALL THE SENSES, AND THE MIRROR PROVIDES A LIVING PICTURE WHICH REFLECTS THE EVER-CHANGING LIGHT.

How many people do you know who seem to be constantly telling their children things like "don't touch that" or "that's dirty, stay away from it" or "don't go outside or you'll muck up your clothes?" If we constantly restrain children from touching natural things because they are not "hygienic," we will create a whole generation that suffers from sensory deprivation. Later on in their lives, this is likely to be reflected in obsessive cleansing routines and a pristine home which looks as if visitors dare not sit down or touch anything. Often these houses are beautiful to look at, but they create a feeling of isolation and introversion amongst the inhabitants.

Your home should be a place where you can delight and develop your sensual enjoyment. It should be bright, clean and airy, and filled with colorful, aromatic and tactile natural products and materials. By introducing a selection of natural objects and materials into the home we can establish the missing connection to the outdoors.

Harmonizing your life with nature

Nature is a like a symphony, formed of harmonious moving patterns of energy. Each one is an instrument, contributing to the whole. For the orchestra to play in tune, each instrument must be tuned to the same note and play in harmony. To bring the orchestra to life, the instruments are designed to create music which is a flow of energy, creating harmonious patterns and cycles.

The forces that govern change in the natural world are mirrored in our minds and bodies. The energy which flows through nature also flows through us affecting our energy levels and internal body rhythms. The quality and type of energy has, therefore, a profound effect on all we think and do.

In the same way that the natural world goes through seasonal cycles of birth, growth, harvesting, and death, we also go through cycles in our life from birth to death. Each season in the cycle of nature has a power and quality and is typified by a certain type of energy. At different stages in our lives, different elements will inevitably come to the fore.

Wood marks the beginning of the creative cycle. It makes things open, firm, and able to carry the load. The wood phase is seen as the birth of life. It takes form when the first fresh yellow-green shoots appear in early spring. These contain the dynamic power of upward movement and growth. The parallel in our lives is the time when we are starting something new and exciting.

The next phase is linked to the heat and energy of the midsummer sun and is known as the fire phase. The heat of this fire energy gives us burning enthusiasm for what we are doing and our own energy levels are high. Late summer is a beautiful time of ripening and flowering. It is the start of the earth phase in the seasonal cycle. The colors are rich and vibrant. It is a relaxed but busy time of year when flowers turn to fruits. In our lives this energy is mirrored as we near the completion of a project and enjoy the fruits of our labors.

Energy starts to slow down and moves downwards as autumn approaches. Seeds fall to the earth, and seek out a place to hide until spring. This part of the cycle is known as the metal phase because metal is generated and created in the center of the earth. In our own lives, this is a time for planning and slowing down.

Winter is a time when nature rests. It is the interval between the movements in nature's symphony. Energy still appears, but it moves in more subtle ways. Winter is the time when we should build up our reserves of strength for the physically active months. This is when we should nurture ourselves and allow ourselves physical rest, while we exercise our minds. It is the perfect time to allow our unconscious to come to the fore, assessing and reflecting on the year gone by and giving us guidance for the future.

In order to sustain and feed these phases, life-giving energy needs to circulate through our homes, nourishing the five elements which in turn feed the corresponding elements in our bodies.

Finding your element

There are few things in life as satisfying as the feeling of really being at home. A house which is the right place for you is something so special that you should be willing to spend time, effort, and even money to create your personal haven.

It is not only the furnishings and the atmosphere which we instill into our homes that are important, but also the spirit of the buildings themselves. This spirit is found in the elements present in the fabric of the walls, floors, and ceilings, as well as in the overall design and architectural style.

The prominence of particular elements in the environment and buildings in which we live is closely related to our relationship to our home. We naturally feel comfortable in a landscape and house which reflects our elemental personality, but feel drained and unhappy in a home where there is a predominance of a destructive energy for us.

Your home has its own character which has developed over a period of time. Like people, every house has a personality. Even a house which is identical in structure and plan to others in the neighborhood will have its own particular quality and power. This will be partly due to its exact location and relationship to the other houses and to the landscape itself.

No two houses are exactly the same. Even if the only obvious difference is the color of the front door, this will give it a special identity. Every house, also has a unique blend of objects and furnishings, and is occupied by different people. All these factors give a home its special personality and ethos.

One of the most interesting ways to discover the unique personality of your home is by assessing the elemental energy present in the building and furnishings. You will also need to look at the elemental personality of the occupiers and see whether the two support and harmonize with one another. Often this affinity happens quite naturally, since we are drawn to places and homes which resonate with the type of energy in our systems.

Before you can discover whether your home is aiding or hindering your life, you need to discover which elemental forces are strong within your own body. The relationship of the elemental forces inside you will reveal themselves in several ways. They will influence your body type and coloring as well as your emotional and mental outlook.

Our personality type is closely linked to the five elements as each of us reflects the strengths and talents representing each element. There are several ways to discover your elemental type, and you may find out that there is more than one element active within your system.

The elements which are most prominent within your system will determine your physique and natural coloring. They will also be reflected by your mental and emotional state, your interests, and your general outlook on life.

The following chapters reveal the numerous ways you can enhance and balance the five elements in order to create a harmonious home with which you are in tune.

Your Birth Year is linked to the five elements. If you were born in a year ending:

0	you are yang metal
1	you are yin metal
2	you are yang water
3	you are yin water
4	you are yang wood
5	you are yin wood
6	you are yang fire
7	you are yin fire
8	you are yang earth
9	you are yin earth

A yin personality is more introverted and you will experience the world more through your thoughts and feelings. Yang personalities are more extraverted and you will express your elemental qualities more through your actions and responses.

By tuning in to the various elements at different times you will be able to receive the right type of energy you require in order to cope with the challenges and changes confronting you:

■ FIRE Assists you in coping with change.

■ EARTH Helps ground you and brings a feeling of security.

■ METAL Enables you to focus on one specific project or aim at a time.

■ WATER Allows you to express your feelings and to go with the flow.

■ WOOD Helps you to stick to your principles and stay true to yourself.

■ Wood people thrive in a wood and fire environment.

■ The water element supports the wood person.

■ The metal element controls imbalances in the wood personality.

WOOD

The pioneer: the archetypal wood personality

Wood is synonymous with spring growth. It is the first element in the natural cycle, and is a powerful force facilitating transformation and change. Assertiveness and a fierce independence are therefore the most important character traits of a wood person. The forcefulness of this element provides muscular strength, and a square physique. The wood person will have strong, slim, or sinewy hands and feet.

Wood personalities are characterized by their determination through action, and a constant striving to surpass their limits. They have ambition, optimism and a conviction that all obstacles can be overcome in the pursuit of their aims. Wood people have strong minds and are decisive, clear, bold, and sometimes aggressive. While the element of wood suggests strength of will and character, it also brings a certain amount of flexibility. So wood people are able to adapt to the circumstances in which they find themselves so long as the environment allows them to grow and change.

If the elements in wood personalities are not in harmony, they may suffer from impatience and intolerance. Their emotions are likely to be volatile and they may suffer from headaches, high blood pressure, and are likely to become dependent on stimulants and sedatives. Wood types need to modulate their intensity and stay flexible, for their strength lies in their ability to adapt under pressure.

Wood people thrive in landscapes which are wooded or forested. They feel comfortable if they have trees in their yard or their home overlooks a park or tree. Natural wood in the home is essential for a wood person, although too much wood may intensify any physical and mental problems they may have.

Metal chops wood in the destructive cycle, so a house with too much metal will be uncomfortable and restrictive for a wood person. Water nourishes wood in the creative cycle, so a house near water or one which contains a water feature will encourage the strengths and talents of the wood element.

Wood is not only beautiful to look at, it also provides us with a multi-dimensional sensory experience. Pale woods are more calming to our emotions, while rich deep colors glow with warmth and vigor. Old wood invariably reminds us of age and history, encouraging us to reflect on and appreciate times gone by. Knotted grains represent growth under pressure and their beauty lies in flowing but contained patterns. Inlaid wood and marquetry are strongly connected with the skill of the craftsman and our mastery over wood. Having a wooden object or piece of furniture made in such a way allows us to appreciate the clarity of thought and commitment that wood inspires in us.

THIS COMFORTABLE ROOM DISPLAYS THE BOLDNESS, HONESTY, AND CLARITY OF WOOD. IT IS ALSO AN ADAPTABLE SPACE WHICH ALLOWS FLEXIBILITY OF LIVING.

FIRE

The communicator: the archetypal fire personality

Fire people are highly sensual and passionate. They relish excitement and drama. They have a love of hot, bright, and vibrant colors, enjoy sensual pleasures, and the good things in life. The unpredictability of this element makes fire people highly intuitive and empathetic. They have a love of life and can bring a sense of joy and light into the darkest places.

Their physical characteristics are those of softness and flexibility. They may be tall with a willowy physique, and graceful hands and feet. They have soft, moist, and supple skins and may have a long neck, arms, and legs.

When the fire element is out of balance these people may experience anxiety, agitation, or even frenzy. They are likely to suffer from nervous exhaustion and insomnia. Physical problems relating to trapped heat in the body may also occur, and may reveal themselves as rashes, sweats, or palpitations. Fire people need to remember to conserve their resources as well as sharing them with others.

A fire person will thrive in a warm, moist climate and a natural environment. Too much water will inhibit fire, but dryness will also deplete fire energy. So fire personalities need homes which have a good balance between fire and water. When the fire element is overstimulated, they need to increase the water element. If their energy is depleted energy, they should seek out the supportive force of wood.

A characteristic trait of the fire element is the need to rise above any self-interest and to give service and healing to others. A home where the fire and water elements are equally present will help these people to find balance between self-interest and the needs of others.

As the fire personality is passionate, these people must be in surroundings which provide intimacy and pleasure. Their attraction to fantastic, exciting, and unusual things means that fire people need constant sensory and mental stimulation, so they like to rearrange furniture and change decor all the time. You will know that you are in a home belonging to a fire personality when there is a sense of the theatrical and the rooms are filled with sensuous textures and fluid shapes. In this rich environment, fire personalities can act out their fantasies and dreams.

The fire home reinforces the optimistic and communicative characteristics of the fire psyche, although to others this type of home may look disorganized and confused. Fire can be fueled with wood so when these two powerful elements are strong, they will exaggerate the fire tendency towards the bizarre or the sentimental. On the other hand, a wood environment can calm highly anxious or stressed fire personalities, bringing stability and direction to their lives. The orderliness, structure, and definition of metal makes fire people feel trapped, so they should avoid homes where metal is too evident.

- Fire people thrive in fire and earth environments.

- The wood element supports the fire person.

- The water home controls imbalances in a fire personality.

THE FIRE ELEMENT IS ALWAYS FULL OF DRAMA AND SURPRISE. THESE STEPPED RED ROOFS SUGGEST THE ERRATIC, LEAPING MOVEMENT OF FIRE, CARRYING ITS ENERGY ALONG THE STREET.

EARTH

The peacemaker: the archetypal earth personality

Most of us know an earth mother. This does not have to be a woman, but applies to anyone who has a protective and nurturing aura. These are the people you go to for help or for a shoulder to cry on. Just being in the company of an earth person gives you a feeling of comfort and well-being.

Unification is the central principle guiding the earth element. This gives people with a strong earth element the power to mediate and promote lasting and peaceful relationships. Earth people are caring and sympathetic, and their inherent stability gives out a feeling of trustworthiness and loyalty.

Earth people like to be in control, without seeking the limelight, because they want to be needed and involved. Their relationships are typified by a wish for harmony and togetherness, so they avoid confrontations and outward displays of anger. As a result earth people tend to bottle up their feelings and have a tendency to be worriers. When the earth element is out of balance they may become overprotective of loved ones and can be seen to be meddlers in other people's affairs. If the earth element is understimulated, the earth person may suffer from low self-esteem and feelings of self-doubt.

Earth people have rounded but firm physiques. They are likely to be large in stature with broad hips and shoulders. Their hands and feet may seem small in proportion to their body. Their faces are often round and their skin is probably peachy smooth and soft.

Earth personalities need an environment where they can balance their desire for a stable relationship with time for themselves. They need the opportunity for self-expression in order to boost their self-confidence.

The home is very important to the earth person, because they need a place of permanence if they are to thrive. Comfort is the most important factor for earth types. They can make for a cozy home in any circumstances, so long as they are surrounded by soft, tactile, and sensual surfaces, as well as objects which they love. Earth personalities are less concerned with style than with the subtle and stable atmosphere of their home.

Attention and intention characterize earth people. They love to remember, so it is quite common to find photos, mementoes, postcards or plaques decorated with their favorite sayings adorning walls, doors, or mantelpieces. As sociability and nurturing are two strong traits of the earth personality, the kitchen is the heart of their home and a place where they can indulge in their desire to make the perfect family.

An earth person will thrive in an earth home. However, the stimulation of the fire element will help boost self-confidence and dispel any fears so a fire home can provide them with the support they need. Fire will help to overcome the earth person's tendency to worry and self-doubt. Earth people will not be able to relax and be themselves in a metal house, while a water home will have a disturbing effect on their lives. Introducing an aspect of the water element will help an earth person to release control and to go with the flow.

IN THIS AFRICAN-INSPIRED ROOM, EARTHENWARE POTS AND EARTH PIGMENTS HAVE BEEN USED TO ENHANCE THE HOMELY AND COMFORTABLE ATMOSPHERE. THIS ENVIRONMENT GENERATES A FEELING OF BEING WELL GROUNDED AND DOWN TO EARTH.

■ An earth person thrives in earth or wood environments.

■ A fire home can provide support for the earth person.

■ The water element can help an earth person to become more flexible.

METAL

The thinker: the archetypal metal personality

You know when you have met a metal person because he or she will be thin and wiry. Physically, the metal element reveals itself in people who are erect, upright, and with a light build. They will have delicate features, with small bones, compact muscles, and a fine, clear, and smooth skin. Often metal people have their hair cut in short, severe, or spiky upright styles to express their natural element.

Metal people are very clever. They are likely to have very analytical minds and reasoned ways of thinking rather than leanings towards creativity. It is hard to get close to metal people as they are fiercely independent and self-reliant. By nature they are not good communicators, but prefer to work out problems on their own.

The guiding principle for the metal element is one of transmutation, because in order for it to be useful, most metal objects have to undergo a process of great change. Metal personalities, therefore, have great powers of discernment, being able to root out insincerity and falsehood. They are people with an ability to find good and a positive side to everything, and are continually striving to create order out of chaos.

Metal types are characterized by their orderliness and methodical approach to life. They are extremely practical and keep everything tidy and in its place. Metal people are more likely to listen to reason and use their minds, than allow their hearts to rule their lives. In the home, the metal person shows a reverence for beautiful objects, ceremony, and refinement.

When the metal element is unbalanced either internally or in the environment, the metal person will suffer from indifference and inhibition. They may become strict and fastidious, paying attention to the smallest details. At worst, they may become obsessive and perform repetitive routines around the house. The metal element is subject to injury from dryness so it is not unusual for the metal type to be prone to a dry skin and stiffness in the back or neck. It is essential that this person does not live in a home where the air is exceptionally dry. This is especially important in winter when many houses are centrally heated.

The home for metal personalities is a place where they can display their need to maintain the highest of standards. They will make their home a place of reverence, beauty, and refinement, carefully choosing furniture and furnishings with style, line, and form in mind. Every object will be kept in a well-defined place. A home which is untidy, or where things get moved around, makes metal personalities feel uncomfortable, and living in such a place will exaggerate their tendencies towards being formal and distant.

Homes which have a strong metal element will help metal people shape and refine their lives. Introducing the fire element into their living spaces will help to control any tendencies to self-control and encourage more spontaneity and passion.

■ Metal people thrive in metal or water environments.

■ Metal people require support from the earth element.

■ A fire home will enliven a metal personality.

THE METAL PERSONALITY LOVES SIMPLE MINIMAL ROOMS, AND PARTICULARLY THE PURITY OF WHITE WALLS AND FURNISHINGS. IN THIS UNCLUTTERED ROOM THEY CAN DELIGHT IN THE PURE FUNCTION AND FORM OF THE ARCHITECTURE AND SCULPTURAL OBJECTS.

WATER

The philosopher: the archetypal water personality

Water types are typified by a feeling of movement and restlessness. These people have a deep insight, bringing what is hidden to view and uncovering new knowledge. They are usually clever, articulate, and introspective so they are likely to be self-sufficient and self-contained individuals. The water personality is a combination of critic, detective, and philosopher, always seeking new understanding and knowledge.

Water people are difficult to get to know because they like to remain secretive and enigmatic. They enjoy working alone and are happy with their own company. When they form deep relationships, they are loyal and constant. However, if their surface is rippled too much, their emotions can rise up in a raging torrent which is very difficult to control. So the water person needs a calm, loving environment in which to thrive.

Their body type is that of a strong, dense but lean physique. Their shoulders are narrow with wider hips. They have long or large bones with a sculptured head and face. Often they have deep-set eyes, while their fingers and toes are long.

Water people are happy in an environment which allows them to concentrate and conserve. When out of balance, this element causes them to become blunt, direct, and detached. Metal can provide the support the water person needs while wood will help attract more tenderness, sensitivity, and openness.

SHADES OF BLUE ENHANCE THE WATER ELEMENT, HELPING YOU TO RELAX AND BECOME MORE FLEXIBLE SO YOU CAN GO WITH THE FLOW.

- Water people thrive in water and wood environments.

- Water people need the element of metal for support.

- The earth element can stabilize a water personality.

Shared homes

Once you have a good idea of which elemental personality you have, you need to assess which element is dominant in your home. By reading through the following sections on each element you will quickly be able to assess both your external and internal environments. These sections will show you how to enhance your natural element and adjust the balance between your positive and negative character traits.

You should remember that while there is one element which is a destructive force, this can be used to control and balance the negative aspects of your element. So fire will help soften and animate a metal person who is too detached and patronizing, while water will help an overprotective earth person to release their grip.

In homes where there are several people with different elemental personalities, you need to find a personal space for each person where their own element can be enhanced. A bedroom or study is a good place to create a harmonious space for the individual. In shared rooms in the home, you need to balance all the elements (see Harmonizing the Five Elements in Your Home on page 114).

LANDSCAPE

THE FIVE ELEMENTS IN THE LANDSCAPE

From the following list you will see what to do if an element is out of balance in your home:

■ If your home is too drafty or windy, you need to adjust the wood element.

■ If your home is too hot, you need to adjust the fire element.

■ If your home is too damp, you need to adjust the earth element.

■ If your home is too dry, stuffy, or dark, you need to adjust the metal element.

■ If your home is too cold, you need to adjust the water element.

To discover how your environment is affecting your health and well-being, you need to look both at the landscape around your home and the architecture and building materials of your home itself. From these you will be able to deduce what type of energetic environment you are living in, whether it is good for you, and whether there are any adjustments you should make.

Our environment has a great influence on our culture and lifestyle, molding and forming our belief system and our way of life. However, our immediate surroundings are not only of aesthetic value; they are also important because of the physical and psychological effect they have on us.

While we are influenced by the "look" of our surroundings, the landscape is pervaded by a subtle force or energy, Chi, which creates a distinct emotional atmosphere that influences us subconsciously. This subtle environment is largely created by the Chi's movement through the landscape. In some places it is fast and noisy like a fast-flowing river, while at other times it meanders through the landscape in a quiet and thoughtful way. Chi moves along the water courses, through the contours of hills and around natural rock formations. Its movement does not end there, for it permeates our homes and our bodies in a never-ending flow.

As Chi moves, it takes on different guises and qualities of the five elements which can be seen in the different features of the landscape, and it is the interplay between the energy of the five elements which creates a harmonious place to live.

Maintaining the flow of energy through the ancient landscape gives continuity to our lives and imbues us with a sense of history and a feeling of belonging. If we scar and change the contours and lines, we also change the fine balance between the elements with the result that we distort the energetic relationships which enable us to sense that somewhere is a good place to live.

The forces that govern nature and the cycles of change in the external world are duplicated in the human body and mind. Each of the elemental forces brings with it a type of energy which is essential to a healthy home. In its turn, a harmonious home will promote a flow of positive energy into our systems.

If our homes are going to feed and nourish us with healthy vibrations, buildings need to be built in sympathy with the surrounding landscape. Houses need to breathe and allow the elemental energy to pass through them. You will soon know that the flow of Chi is distorted when one of the elements becomes too powerful. This results in your house being very hot or cold, damp or too exposed to the wind and weather. Too much of any particular type of energy will adversely affect the occupants.

If your home is built in a very windy position, it will have an imbalance in the wood element. You need to increase the protective qualities of wood. In this case you could install wooden shutters or build a timber pergola or porch to provide more shelter. If you have a garden, you need to make a windbreak from some hardy trees or a strong timber fence. If your home is drafty, make sure your doors are strong and well fitted and that your windows are double or triple glazed. Adding an entrance porch would also help to minimize drafts.

A cold house will reflect the presence of too much water energy, while a damp house suggests a problem related to the earth energy. If your home is cold, you need to increase the fire energy to warm up your home. Try to create more light by enlarging the windows and installing a working fireplace. A cold house, like a damp house, would benefit from decoration in warm bright colors (make sure the paints are porous). If possible, create a sunroom or add a room on the cold side of the house as this will act as insulation.

Dampness lingers in the air so a dehumidifier is a good investment, but you also need to check the damp-proofing. Homes built from traditional materials were designed without a damp course, so that water would rise from the ground and by a process of osmosis, pass unobstructed through the walls to the outside. If any of the previous owners have interfered with this natural process water will be trapped inside. It could be that they used modern cement to render the walls. This is impermeable to water and, unlike old-fashioned lime mortar, creates damp in the walls. As with the interior, you need to make sure that the outside surfaces of a traditionally constructed house are painted with a permeable paint.

If your house is very hot, the fire element is too strong. You need to find ways of creating a good air flow through your home. Fit soft translucent drapes to the windows on the sunny side of your home, and add some blinds or awnings. Large windows should also have thick drapes to cut out the light during the hottest part of the day. A hot house needs a cool uncluttered interior. Choose tones which remind you of the sparkling ocean or a clear sky, and replace thick carpets and rugs with cool ceramic tiles, stone, or slate flooring.

Identifying the elements

Everyone has a dream place they would like to live, perhaps near the sea or in the mountains, and this is very revealing about which environment is good for you. Ideally, you should be somewhere which is in sympathy with your inner being so that it nurtures your soul and makes you feel at home. But often people get stuck in places which are far from perfect. If this is you, take heart because you can use the harmonizing qualities of the five elements to improve the subtle environment in and around your home.

To discover whether you are living in the right place for you, start by looking at the relationships between the elements. One or two of the natural elements will be prominent in your home. These will depend on the energy flowing through the nearby landscape and on the style of architecture and materials used in the construction.

To discover which elements are flowing through the landscape around your home you should first look at the surrounding area, making note of the elemental shapes you can see. If you live in the country you will be able to find the elements in the natural topography of the area. The wood element manifests itself in high, rounded hills. Metal is found in more steep-sloping sides meeting at a ridge. Anything shaped like a pyramid indicates the fire element, while earth is present in squarer, flat-topped shapes. Water is not only found in lakes, mountains and the ocean but in rolling, gently undulating landscape.

In a city you will be able to find the elemental shapes in the skyline and in buildings. The fire element is linked to churches, spires, steeply pitched roofs, and signposts. Wood is the element present in tall chimneys, fence posts, and towers. Metal is found in roads, rail tracks, pylons, and properties with steep angles, while the earth element is present in square buildings, particularly those with flat roofs. Water can be found in rounded roofs, tunnels, and bridges.

Walking around your neighborhood you will quickly be able to identify one or more of these elements. Ask yourself which ones are present and which are missing. Once you know the type of environment you are dealing with, you can introduce the missing elements to enhance the flow of subtle energy in and around your home. If you are in harmony with the surrounding elements, you can enhance this positive energy inside your home. If you feel uncomfortable, the dominant elements will be at odds with your make-up, so you should introduce the controlling elements and create an interior more suited to your personality.

Make a note of the elemental shapes in the landscape around your home to discover which elements are dominant:

■ Wood is seen in tall, rounded hills with steep upright sides. Also in chimneys, fence posts, lampposts, tall chimney stacks, and towers.

■ Metal is present in sloping sides that meet at a narrow, peaked top, as in mountain peaks and tall pointed pine trees. Pylons, rail tracks, and railings are more obvious indicators of a metal landscape.

■ Fire is found in pyramid shapes, with sloping sides and a pointed top especially churches, spires, steeply pitched roofs, and signposts.

■ Earth is found in square, flat-topped shapes, in box-like buildings and flat roofs.

■ Water is seen in rolling hills and soft undulating landscape, in mall rooftops, rounded roofs, tunnels, and bridges.

THE WOOD ENVIRONMENT

The wood environment is good for a wood or fire personality.
A wood environment will bring new growth and flexibility into your life.
Wood will give strength to a water person.

The wood environment is very powerful yet also subtle. You know you are in a wood environment when you sense a place with strong roots but which also seems to be evolving and growing. It may be somewhere with a sense of history, or its strength may lie in the stability afforded to a place by trees or timber buildings. Whereas a fire environment is one which seems to be changing fast and furiously, the organic changes occurring in the wood environment are much longer lasting and less superficial.

The wood environment is found in many places in towns as well as in the countryside. One of the most notable attractions of the wood environment is that it stays true to itself even when fashioned by tools. Tall trees have a strong presence whether they are in the forest or have been turned into beams or planking. If you are walking through a parkland or forest or sitting around a wooden table at home, wood demands acknowledgement.

In the landscape a strong wood element can afford a householder protection. Trees behind your home stand guard, and will shield against the prevailing winds or a noisy road. The presence of the tree can root you to a place and lend weight to your sense of belonging.

The wood building

Timber homes have heart as they are made from a living product. Even when a tree is cut down and turned into timber, its spirit lives on for hundreds of years. This immortal quality pervades our own system, giving us a special energy and enthusiasm for life. Living in a home with a strong presence of wood is therefore a very special and nurturing experience.

In many warm climates where houses are built from timber, there are no distinct separations between the inside and outside. "Interspaces" which link indoors to outdoors often have timber decking with other open structures, such as fences, arbors, and pergolas. Instinctively the builders recreate the safety of a wooded place and the relaxed security afforded by tall trees.

In Japan, the warm temperate climate resulted in magnificent forests, so it is not surprising that wood has always been favored as the basic building material. Rather than protecting the householder from the weather, the Japanese welcomed the outdoors and nature into their lives. They recognized the importance of grass and trees in creating a feeling of openness and connection with their surroundings. The qualities of unity and connection carried by wood make it a perfect material to use in the construction of sacred spaces. The earliest Buddhist temples and especially Zen shrines were timber structures which opened onto a wooded area or garden.

In other wooded countries, where timber was easily found, cut, and shaped into logs and beams, traditional homes were also made from wood. The timber framework was filled in with a mixture of mud and straw, so that the materials united to form a strong structure which gave good protection against the elements. The strength to weight ratio of timber is far greater than mild steel

WOOD BRINGS STRENGTH AND PERMANENCE TO THE FLEXIBLE AND CHANGEABLE WATER ELEMENT. THIS WOULD BE A GOOD HOME FOR A WATER OR A WOOD PERSON, PROVIDING A CHALLENGING AND CREATIVE ENVIRONMENT.

or reinforced concrete, and compared to its weight, wood is immensely strong.

Wood lasts for a long time, but it does degrade over the years, so many ancient wooden buildings have not survived. The most common early timber-framed houses surviving in the U.K. today were built over four hundred years ago proving the durability of this material. Frequently, however, buildings in the Tudor style of the Elizabethan era are more recent mock-Tudor copies or adaptations. The Victorians were particularly keen on re-creating styles from the past, and so many buildings during the latter part of the nineteenth century have a strong wood presence.

Building with timber was eventually superseded by brick-built dwellings and later on prefabricated materials and concrete blocks. The growing number of houses being built made timber impractical and expensive. Fortunately there is a renewed interest in timber-framed homes and cladding, and homes built from green oak and imported timber grown in sustainable managed forests are springing up. There is now also a whole range of building products made from wood, and one can obtain building blocks and sheets made from pressed waste paper products, sawdust, and wood shavings. The more environmentally conscious architects and designers are also designing roofs which can be covered with real turf, and in many countries individuals are creating gardens on flat roofs.

For centuries children throughout the world have enjoyed the safety and thrills of tree houses, but now garden rooms constructed in trees are becoming so popular that there are building companies specializing in their creation. People are using tree houses as bedrooms, offices, and entertainment areas as well as playrooms. When sympathetically designed and built, this renewed interest in trees may heighten our awareness to the importance of this valuable resource.

Houses with a strong wood element need not be built entirely from timber. Log cabins of all designs and timber-framed buildings naturally reflect the wood element. But even if your home is built from another material, if it is timber clad or the interior has exposed beams your home will be strongly associated with the qualities of wood.

The wood element may be visible in timber cladding or wooden windows or it may be hidden in the roof or floor. Even in the oldest buildings wood was used to make ladders to gain access to the upper stories and roof, and many homes still incorporate timber into a staircase.

A key point to remember is that a home which has a strong wood element needs to have a good supply of earth energy, or the home will not be well rooted and the ideas and plans of the householders are likely to collapse. When you are under pressure from outside forces to change your direction or standpoint, it is helpful to be in a home which features a strong wood element. Being surrounded by wood will give you an inner strength to stick to your principles and keep your integrity. Wood provides a quiet dignity but also has enough flexibility to allow you to see things from different perspectives without losing sight of your judgment.

TREES HAVE A TRANSFORMATIVE ENERGY SINCE THEY CAN TURN CARBON DIOXIDE INTO OXYGEN, THUS KEEPING THE AIR FRESH AND HEALTHY. BEING IN A TREE GIVES YOU A DIFFERENT PERSPECTIVE ON LIFE. IT MAKES YOU FEEL LIGHT AND FREE FROM THE RESTRICTIONS OF THE GROUND AND YOUR NORMAL ROUTINE.

THE EARTH ENVIRONMENT

An earth environment is good for an earth or metal personality.
A water person will be uncomfortable in an earth environment.
The earth element will ground and calm a fire person.

Places where the earth element is strong are not only visible but can also be felt. Low rolling hills and wide valleys give the impression of the landscape embracing and folding its arms around you. These places have a very feminine and nurturing atmosphere and people who live in these surroundings often remain there for long periods of time. There is usually a good flow of other elemental energy in places where the earth element is strong as the climate in earthy places is mild and warm so there is plenty of water and greenery.

When looking at the landscape from the air, areas of strong earth energy will have rounded contours and rivers will meander through the valleys in large rounded loops. In the city, houses which are built around low hills will enjoy the benefits of earth energy. So too will those built in a close (where the grounds are enclosed) or in a crescent-shaped street. Any underlying circular shape affords protection and stability and it has been proved that a circular arrangement creates a strong sense of community, providing one of safest and most neighborly environments in which to live.

Some earth landscapes are much more dynamic. In areas where there has been great geological upheaval, the earth is often exposed in huge rocky outcrops and towering shapes. Many desert and semi-desert areas have such strong earth energy that other elements such as water and wood are totally missing. The earth element will naturally be strong in homes built in these areas. In such situations where the earth element is out of balance, it is essential that the water element is introduced to control it.

While we follow the trend of building houses on "green" sites in the countryside, the speed at which we are losing our earth connection is rapidly increasing because the earth is literally being covered up by buildings. It is only in places where people are aware of the dire consequences of urbanization that action is being taken. The Swiss government has recognized the long-term problems this will cause to both the environment and subsequently to people's physical and mental health. So in 1999 it legislated that new buildings must be designed to relocate the green space covered by the building's "footprint" to the roof. Even historical buildings must now include a rooftop garden on 20 percent of their roof space. Elsewhere in the world, authorities are quickly recognizing that the ozone and climate are being detrimentally affected by a lack of green space and even the roof of Chicago's city hall is to be planted with grass, ivy, and two oak trees in order to reduce air pollution. While the creation of turf roofs and roof gardens is a move in the right direction, the creation of these earth "sandwiches" will have more far-reaching psychological effects. Buildings really need to harmonize with the environment in terms of materials, shape, and scale. Earth buildings fulfill all these criteria, for they appear to rise up out of the earth itself, reinforcing our emotional bonding with our fragile planet.

TO THE NATIVE AMERICAN PEOPLE, THE RED EARTH OF THIS MOUNTAIN IN UTAH WAS SYMBOLIC OF THE SUNRISE, LIGHT, AND LIFE ITSELF. THE EARTH ENVIRONMENT CREATES A DIMENSION WHICH PINPOINTS LOCATION IN TIME AND SPACE, GIVING A FEELING OF AGE AND PERMANENCE.

The earth building

The earth home is very much part of its environment, and one of its main features is its smooth organic form. These buildings appear to rise up naturally from the ground and blend into the landscape with ease. True earth houses are literally made from the earth, baked mud, or a mixture of clay and straw. The very nature of this building method results in a home that has no hard straight lines. So houses with a strong earth connection are often round in shape or have curved walls, with the floor and walls merging together. The finishing touch to an earth home may be a roof of thatch, clay tiles, or even turf.

Earth has always been the most basic and easily accessible building material available to us and one which allows us to express our innate creativity. Its wonderful consistency makes it easy to transport and mold into various shapes suitable for building houses. Mud was used in the most ancient form of dwellings where it was mixed with water and straw to become a pliable substance which was smeared over a framework of timber, stone, or rammed into frames. When earth is used as a building material it has excellent temperature moderating properties, so that the interior of the home is cool in summer and warm in winter. Although many traditional buildings were once made with a mixture of clay and straw, raw earth is rarely used today although there is a renewed interest in this type of building method.

Earth houses were not only simple to build but were easy to maintain since the inside and outside became an integral unit. In a structure where the walls, floors, and ceilings are continuous, little dirt and dust can collect, making earth houses easy to clean. Often an earth building will incorporate furniture, storage, and cooking facilities in the fabric of the home itself, so that one can sit on smooth low walls or place storage containers in alcoves and holes. This makes living in an earth building a very sensual and interactive experience. Interior fittings such as beds, fireplaces, and storage areas were often created at the time of building, avoiding the need for furniture. Fired earth also frequently provided the basic utensils needed for cooking. A simple and exciting way of experiencing the qualities of molded earth is by building a pizza or bread oven into your patio or kitchen area. The smooth organic form has a large rounded base and a smooth, funnel-shaped chimney that resembles the fullness of a sun-ripened squash.

Fired earth is a more familiar building material than raw earth. Sun-baked blocks and bricks have been used in building construction for centuries and today we still rely on baked bricks as a convenient and flexible building material for our homes. Fired bricks create a strong but living, breathing material which is in perfect harmony with the earth from where it comes. Under foot, hand-baked terracotta tiles resemble the naturally undulating surface of the ground which enhances our earth connection when we walk on them with bare feet. Handmade bricks and tiles have their own individual coloring, each tile blending in with the next to generate an earthy, warm, and subtle effect. Use them when you wish to create a more relaxed and casual lifestyle.

In addition to whether or not a home is made from fired clay bricks, the overall shape of the building will indicate whether the earth element is strong. A house with a good earth connection will sit squarely on the ground. It will give the impression that it rises up from the earth, rather than being dumped onto it. Even if your home is not made from earth building materials, the inside may reveal a strong earth connection.

EARTH BUILDINGS BLEND INTO THE LANDSCAPE AS IF THEY HAVE GROWN OUT OF THE EARTH ITSELF. THEY CREATE AN AURA OF PERMANENCE AND APPEAR ROOTED TO THE SPOT. HOMES LIKE THESE HAVE BEEN BUILT IN THIS WAY WITH LITTLE CHANGE OVER THOUSANDS OF YEARS.

THE METAL ENVIRONMENT

A metal environment and home is good for metal and water personalities.
A metal home is destructive for a wood personality, and a neutral place for a
fire person.

The metal environment is one of striking contrasts, which can be either natural or manmade. In Chinese philosophy and especially in the art of feng shui, the metal element is typified by its sharp angles and pointed shapes. In some places these shapes occur naturally in the landscape. Mountains which have sharp peaks, of which the Mattahorn on the Swiss–Italian border is a good example, reveal a strong metal element. As this element is also linked to coldness and the color white, the snow covering such high mountains enforces the metal character. Pointed cone-shaped trees which grow high on the slopes help carry the metal element through the landscape. Sometimes these dark green trees appear black, and when they are covered with snow, the contrast is dramatic and striking.

Indications of metal in the environment are not only tall and vertical, they can be horizontal lines too. Rail tracks that cover vast distances, electric pylons and power lines crisscrossing the countryside all point to a strong presence of metal. Metal bridges spanning rivers also carry the metal element through the landscape, supporting the water element with which it has an affinity.

Deep underground lie seams of rocks and minerals that give out strong impulses of energy so often a place is transversed by a strong metal energy of which we are unaware. To give an example, the area around the farm on which I grew up in southern Africa used to suffer from frequent violent electric storms. It was quite common for lightning to strike the ground all around the house and in the garden. The reason for this was that the hill contained minerals which attracted the electrical current. Later I came to appreciate that fire is nature's way of controlling the strong metal element in the earth, and that the thunderstorms are necessary to maintain this balance.

In the urban environment not only are there minerals and rocks below ground, there are also vast numbers of wires, cables, and pipes, many of which are made from metal. Often we can only sense the presence of metal intuitively. Perhaps a particular place has a strong sense of focus and it may draw you to it like a magnet.

The more obvious metal environment is visible and above ground. Most modern towns and cities have buildings and many other structures made from metal. In industrial areas, whole buildings and roofs may be metal, and most streets have an abundance of railings, trash bins, street lamps and traffic signs made from this material.

The metal building

Although many ancient civilizations had the ability to mine and manufacture metals, it is only in recent times that we have been able to do this is large enough quantities to incorporate metal into our building structures.

Throughout history, metals have been used to adorn buildings decoratively, but towards the end of the eighteenth century metal began to be manufactured on a grand scale. Since then, metal has been favored as a building material for its adaptability and strength. Homes were built with ornate verandas, balconies, and conservatories. In the early twentieth century, metal was reserved for public buildings such as railway stations and large industrial factories but later it was used to create multi-story housing and offices. Today metal is still

IT IS ESSENTIAL THAT THE OCCUPANTS OF THIS METAL
MOBILE HOME ARE HIGHLY ORGANIZED AND TIDY. BOTH
THESE QUALITIES ARE INSPIRED BY THE METAL ELEMENT.

a popular material for all kinds of buildings in both the public and private sectors.

Even in older buildings over three stories high, metal beams are often introduced, and you might find a reinforced steel joist (RSJ) in your basement or where an old doorway or window has been enlarged. The growing trend for reclaiming old warehouses and commercial buildings has also led to more people living in buildings where the metal element is prominent. Even if you don't live in a building with a metal structure, many modern houses have RSJs that support loadbearing walls. On a smaller scale around the home, garden rooms and sheds are often made from metal or have metal components. If your home has a concrete staircase or stands on concrete pylons, these, too, are likely to have reinforcing steel running through them. So even if you have a house in which another element is dominant, it is helpful to remember that metal is very likely to be present, even if it is not obvious at first glance.

Architectural styles can also reflect the metal element. Usually these buildings are tall and unadorned. They are often modern in design and have a simplicity which focuses attention on the materials used. For this reason, the materials in steel and concrete buildings are usually exposed in their natural state but they will not have a stronger metal energy than those which have been rendered or painted. If you live in a building with a central shaft, this will have a strong metal presence, as will those homes with prominent metal railings, gates, and burglar guards.

Many churches and shrines are pervaded with the spirit of metal. This is especially strong in buildings which are have pointed towers and steeples. Gothic architecture reflects a strong metal influence, and like high peaks on a mountain, the soaring lines of Gothic stonework draw our attention upwards to a point of focus above. Homes with towers and steep gables have a similar effect. In such places the metal element can create a quiet sanctuary, where we can concentrate fully on the spiritual aspects of life.

One style of architecture which had a great sympathy for the metal element occurred during the 1930s. Art Deco typifies the sharp clean lines and qualities of metal. Buildings erected during this time often had metal windows and stairs, and purpose-built apartments were fitted with elevators with folding metal doors. During this period interior design made great use of black and white which created strong contrasts and dramatic themes. Other popular features included shiny tiles, mirrored surfaces, and leaded windows.

If you live (permanently or ocasionally) in a mobile home or camper, you may find the metal element has become too powerful because this is the predominant construction material. To redress the balance you need to increase the fire element somehow. Rather than making a small space hot and uncomfortable, it is better (and just as effective) to invoke the fire element through symbolic rather than physical means (see Harmonizing the Five Elements in Your Home on page 114).

THE WATER ENVIRONMENT

The water environment and home are good for water and wood personalities.
A water environment will dampen the spirits of a fire person.
Water will bring flexibility and help a metal person to loosen up.

The dramatic role of water in our lives makes it one of the main elemental influences in the landscape. Comprising oxygen and hydrogen, water is the most abundant compound found on earth. When considering the landscape, the water element is not only present in seas, lakes and rivers, but also in the air and in the formation of the earth itself. In Chinese mythology, the great water dragons are believed to reveal themselves in the contours of the hills and mountains, and can be found in the undulating shapes of vegetation, walls, and buildings.

In much earlier times, settlers often built their homes in close proximity to water that provided for their essential needs. Moving water brings with it great vitality, and those settlements near an inlet, a river, or the sea soon developed into busy trading stations. Today, all over the world, waterside properties still remain the most desirable, as most people enjoy the benefits from the refreshing and uplifting properties of this element.

Communities are often strongly bonded when they live near water, which acts as a central focus and unifying agent, and in my experience this is certainly true. I live in a small market town which straddles the head of a navigable river. The river is the heart of the town, around which the lives of many of the residents revolve. My fellow townspeople are especially community minded and the spirit of the river really seems to bring us together.

There are two types of water environments, and they are linked to still and flowing water. The first water environment conveys a place of safety as it evokes our primordial memories of living in the sea and being suspended in fluid in the womb. The rounded hills and forms nurture and protect us. The landscape will feel open and light, its flowing horizontal lines will be natural and unbroken, without the harshness often found in places where other elements dominate.

The second water environment links to moving water, conveying a feeling of movement and change. This is especially strong in places which are close to the sea or a tidal or fast-flowing river. These places are seldom threatening and the movement of the water creates a healing environment which enlivens and refreshes the spirit. The movement of water is able to shift energy in our physical and subtle bodies (the energy from our thoughts, emotions, and spiritual essences). Water also creates its own positive energy in the form of negative ions which pervade the surroundings and generate an abundance of life-force energy.

Moving water is perfect for shifting pollutants in the atmosphere and its sound can mask noise from roads, factories, and machinery. When I was visiting a Japanese garden in the middle of Tokyo, I discovered a beautiful place to sit next to a waterfall which had been created alongside a stand of tall bamboo. It was only when I ventured further along the path that I realized that there was a three-tier highway effectively concealed behind the bamboo. The traffic's roar had been drowned by the sound of the waterfall.

The earth is permeated by underground rivers and water courses, and places where there is moving energy below ground have a special quality. Many sacred sites are located at the source of natural springs and pools, while houses that are built over underground streams literally bubble with energy. In England and other places which have a warm temperate climate, there is usually so much ground water that there are few properties which do not benefit from the positive qualities of the water element. In the natural creative cycle, water feeds wood and so in places where there is a good flow of water, there will also be an abundance of timber. Wood helps to stabilize the moving flow of water.

There are, however, some places where water can have a negative effect on the house occupants. Water is a carrier of electro-magnetic energy, which builds up as it is forced through underground fissures and over rocks. This flow creates a static electric field which can disturb the earth's electro-magnetic field at that point. Houses built on such sites can often become "unhealthy" because the water can interfere with the magnetic fields running through our bodies. This can result in disturbances of the nervous system and electrical patterns in the brain. The ill effects are only likely to become apparent if people spend a great deal of time in such a building.

The water building

Water buildings have a quiet and peaceful quality but they can also reflect the strength and power of the oceans. By nature, water is obviously not a suitable building material but many homes and offices are built near water and take on the fluidity of this element. Glass has the same reflective qualities as water and is often used to conjure up this aspect. Curved roofs and spirals also convey the movement of waves and ocean currents. Water buildings may be circular and incorporate curved and snake-like shapes. Even if they have a more regular layout, a water building is usually quite low with strong horizontal lines.

If your home is built near water or in a low-lying area, it will have a good supply of water energy. Converted water mills have the water element literally flowing right through them, while beach cottages, houseboats and homes with moorings, and boat houses also carry water energy.

As the water element is so intertwined with our emotions, relationships are the key to the water home. The water home is likely to be an older style and more traditionally built home. Even in modern houses, the water home is likely to have a friendly, old-fashioned feel to it. Traditional Scandinavian architecture reflects the water element particularly well. These houses are simple, homely, and decorated in tones of watery blues, greens, and shimmering off-white. Shaker-style homes also contain a simple elegance, which reflects the tranquillity and serenity of the water element.

Water houses are natural and comfortable. Their forms are created from the materials themselves, so that there is no pretence. This sense of honesty pervades the style and objects filling the water home. Instead of carefully organized and symmetrical arrangements, the water element winds its way through the house without any formal sense of order. Changes and additions to a water home occur when they are needed, which is why many water homes have additions and alterations made to them in a rather haphazard way. Often it is only after our home is built that we feel a need to introduce the water element. Fountains and other water features add a final sparkle and bring soothing qualities which seem to make our homes complete.

HERE THE WATER ELEMENT IS CONTAINED WITHIN A WOODEN BUILDING, REMINDING US THAT WATER NOURISHES OUR OWN BODIES, LIKE SAP WITHIN A TREE. PEOPLE HAVE A NATURAL BUOYANCY IN WATER. BY TAKING A DIP IN AN INDOOR POOL, WE KEEP OURSELVES HEALTHY AND ALSO FEEL EMOTIONALLY SUPPORTED.

THE FIRE ENVIRONMENT

The fire element is good for fire or wood personalities,
but it is uncomfortable for a metal person.
The fire element stimulates creativity and a zest for life.

Fire and heat go hand in hand. So it is not difficult to see why hot dry places are linked to the fire element. Homes built on volcanic rock or near an active volcano are full of fire energy. If you live in a sunny dry place, your home will also be permeated by this fiery element. The risk of fire is always great in these areas and so the inhabitants are very aware of the power of the fire element. In a home dominated by the fire element, it is essential that the water element is introduced to counterbalance and control the fire. If you live in a hot and humid location, the fire element will still be strong, but the water in the atmosphere will ensure that the fire element is controlled.

The fire element is characterized by sharp angles, irregular shapes, and triangles, so if your house is built on a plot set out in one of these plans, the fire energy will flow into your home. This also applies to buildings which are built in between two roads or at the place where two rivers meet at a sharp angle.

Areas which are undergoing change are likely to fall under the fire element. It may be that the area where you live is being developed or altered in some way. Places which are built on reclaimed land, or where there has been a major change of use, fall under this category. So if you have moved to a building which was not created for residential use, this metamorphosis will indicate the presence of fire energy.

THE SOARING CURVED ROOFS OF THESE BUILDINGS IN MALAYSIA EMBODY THE CAPACITY OF THE FIRE ELEMENT TO LIFT OUR SPIRITS AND ALLOW US TO MAKE A LEAP FORWARD IN OUR LIVES.

The fire building

Fire buildings are dramatic and eye-catching so it is difficult to walk past them without being impressed. The sun theme has been used by builders and architects throughout history and today we are still fascinated by the powerful force of the fiery sun.

Shapes are strongly linked to the five elements and in the case of fire, these are expressed as sharp angles and any unexpected juxtaposition of different forms. If buildings are pointed and tall, fire energy will be even more pronounced. It is not unusual for them to be crowned with a pyramid roof or to have a sunburst feature over the main entrance. The pyramid shape is especially linked to the fire element because this structure is imbued with mystical powers of transformation and regeneration.

Some buildings are directly connected to light and fire and these buildings are gaining popularity for conversion into living spaces. Lighthouses and old fire stations were closely associated with creating and controlling fire, so that these places remain highly charged with fire energy. Fortunately lighthouses overlook the sea, so in these buildings the water element acts as a controlling force.

The close connection between the fire element and the spirit or divine spark is revealed in any structure which points to the heavens. This is why so many churches contain fire energy. The most powerful of these were built during the Gothic period, where buildings soar toward the sky with steeply pointed roofs and spires. When the sun's rays shine through their stained-glass windows, these churches are flooded with colored light which increases the effect of the fire element. A softer version of this fire energy can be found in the onion-shaped domes of Russian and some Greek Orthodox churches. In these buildings the onion domes and spires resemble candle flames, and are especially inspiring when their rich tiles and mosaics sparkle in sunlight.

Today, modern architecture often carries a strong fire element. Buildings which have a strong masculine energy are often large and imposing in comparison with neighboring property. These buildings can be constucted out of many different materials, but the overall feeling is one of hardness and strength. These homes are often shocking and disturbing to look at with sharp angles and asymmetrical shapes, so that they never appear to be quite still. This agitation reflects the fire element well, as it is quite different in quality to the composed symmetry of many older building styles. Fire buildings are full of drama and surprise and sometimes they have gold-tinted windows or reflective surfaces which catch the light. If you have stained-glass windows in your home, these too, will amplify the fire energy from the sun.

Architecturally, the fire element lends itself to structures that point upwards incorporating geometric shapes and sharp angles. The roof of a fire home is often steeply pitched and a good indication that the element is dominant. Typical examples are the upswept roofs, reminiscent of flames, found in China and Malaysia, A-framed houses of all types, but especially Scandinavian and Swiss, and traditional longhouses and barns. Traditional timber barns painted in a rich dark red, found in Vermont and in many parts of New England, are also fire buildings. Whatever its style, a red-colored house will attract the fire element and its energy, and will also influence the immediate neighborhood.

PYRAMID SHAPES ARE RENOWNED FOR THE SURPRISING ENERGY THAT THEY CREATE. VIEWING THIS BUILDING FROM INSIDE OR OUT, YOUR SPIRIT SOARS UPWARDS SO THAT YOU FEEL CHANGED IN SOME WAY. FIRE ENERGY HAS TRANSFORMATIVE AND REJUVENATING QUALITIES.

Public and private spaces

Public buildings are for show; they serve as monuments and beacons, in addition to their perceived role of providing space where the public and local community can gather for a variety of reasons. We seldom spend long periods of time in these places and this allows architects to design buildings which embody the qualities of one particular element. It does not take long, however, before we feel uncomfortable in such a space, and it is likely that the energy generated by the dominant element will cause us distress if we spend too much time there.

In contrast to public buildings, it is essential that we feel comfortable in places which we inhabit regularly. Most buildings contain a mixture of elemental materials and qualities but your home will undoubtedly express one of the elements more strongly than the others. As your home is your private space where you should feel relaxed and at one with your environment, it is vital that you feel an affinity with your surroundings. So always make sure that you live in an environment which mirrors the elemental energy running through your life (this may change from time to time).

Knowledge of how the natural elements have molded society as a whole makes it easier to appreciate how powerful the elements can be in shaping the lives of individuals.

WOOD

WOOD

Physical attributes: strength, suppleness, expansion, acceleration
Mental attributes: clarity, judgment, foresight, decision
Compass direction: east
Home power center: living room or kitchen

The spirit of wood

The tree is the supreme natural symbol of dynamic growth, seasonal death, and regeneration. Its elemental properties are those of pushing to the limits, finding its own space and light, and survival under pressure.

Throughout history the tree has been viewed as providing the axis through which divine energy flows from the supernatural to the natural world. Mythology of the tree is universal and in many cultures the tree is seen to be rooted in the underworld, passing through the earth and ending in the heavens. In some traditions it grows on a sacred mountain or in Paradise, while others see a fountain of spiritual nourishment gushing from its roots. When a snake is coiled at its base, it suggests spiraling energy drawn from the earth.

The shape of a tree provides the ideal form to portray the evolution of the soul, for through the Tree of Life, humanity ascends from the lower levels toward spiritual illumination. The trunk can be seen as the unifying force while the branches suggest diversity spreading out in all directions. Different types of trees are considered the Tree of Life in different cultures. In Egypt it is the weeping fig, and in Middle Eastern traditions it is the olive, palm, or pomegranate. Sometimes the fruit from the Tree of Life has been portrayed as stars, moons, and planets, while in China the fruits symbolize immortality.

Wood marks the beginning of the creative cycle. It makes things open, firm, and capable of carrying a load. The dynamic growth of the tree makes the wood element align with the season of spring which represents the dawn of awakening.

The compass direction linked to the element of wood is the east, where the sun rises.

The wood element can assist you in finding new challenges and achieving your goals. It will help you to enjoy working under pressure and encourage a love of action and adventure. Wood will fix mercurial qualities in your character but may intensify the tendency toward materialism.

The power of wood comes from its capacity for rapid expansion while staying flexible and able to yield where necessary. Above all, it will bring with it a new enthusiasm for life.

The wood element in the home

Wood brings strength and dignity to your home. It symbolizes the change in our value system from that of the material to the spiritual. The wood element creates an atmosphere of comfort and tranquillity which echoes our inner needs, reflecting the idea that progress and efficiency should be valued above all else.

The wood element can take many guises, not only in timber but in other plants too. If you wish to enhance the wood element in the home, you need to consider three distinct qualities of the plant kingdom and find appropriate objects to suggest these.

The first aspect of wood is that of unity and strength, which is symbolized by the tree trunk. If you wish to introduce the strength and dignity of this element, it is best to choose large pieces of timber. Wooden floors, beams, wall panels, and furniture will make an immediate impact in a home where the wood element is in short supply. Whenever possible, it is always better to select old or used timber for this purpose because it will be of a better quality, and we should also try to recycle this rapidly dwindling resource.

If you buy modern timber, especially hardwood, you should check first that it doesn't come from tropical rainforests. There are a large number of sustainable hardwood forests being created as a renewable resource, producing a wide range of beautiful woods including oak, elm, maple, apple, beech, walnut, and sycamore. The darker the color of the wood in your home, the more power and strength it will summon.

Timber from trees is not the only source of powerful wood energy, for it is beaten by the strength to weight ratio of bamboo. When I was in Hong Kong, I remember marveling at bamboo scaffolding erected on the outside of multi-storied steel buildings while they were being constructed. By comparison, the bamboo structure looked very flimsy and yet it was quick and easy to erect compared to its metal counterpart, as well as being very strong.

The second quality of the wood element is that of flexibility and elegance. Wood can help you to appreciate beauty in everything, and is especially good for helping you to focus on the simple and joyful things in life. These qualities can be created by including in your home a wealth of small objects made from small trees, bamboo, grasses, and leaf fibers. The flexible stems of these plants are thin and upright but they have a great degree of movement. Trees such as the aspen, elder, and birch dance gracefully in the wind, and so would also be a good choice of material. Lighter colored wood of all types carries the suggestion of subtlety and flexibility which is found in all trees.

The third quality of wood is conveyed by its many branches, leaves, flowers, and fruits. This bountiful array brings the variety and the abundance of nature into your home. Materials like jute, sisal, hemp, and coir make wonderful floor coverings which contribute to warm and evocative living spaces. Raffia, rattan, and honey-colored

bamboo canes are comforting materials that lend themselves well to a range of furniture, blinds, and screens that boost the wood energy.

Another option is to create your own decorative objects out of bark, paper, and leaves. Try making a delicate mobile from driftwood or cover decorative boxes with handmade paper and bark.

Bringing wood into your living room can imbue your home and your family with a feeling of strength and dignity. While your personal relationships may be strong, the wood element will allow flexibility and movement, enabling your love to withstand hardship and stress. Wood symbolizes rapid growth and transformation, and if you bring this element into your home you will help to promote changes in your life.

In the kitchen, the energy of wood brings you close to nature and the appreciation of fresh natural food. Its message is one of abundance and nourishment of the body and spirit. In the bathroom, the wood element can create a relaxing atmosphere where you honor and enjoy a connection with nature. Timber is a warm and comforting material to touch, and if you introduce timber into your bathing environment, it will provide a tranquil and nurturing experience. Similarly, you will find that walking barefoot on a smooth wooden floor is warming and soothing.

If you have ever spent a night out of doors in a wood or among trees, you will know that the spirit of wood can be very frightening after dark. Tall trees block out the sky and can create a feeling of foreboding. Too much wood in the bedroom can mimic this environment, with the result that the room might begin to feel claustrophobic and oppressive. This is why it is better to use lighter and more delicate forms of the wood element in the bedroom. Soft greens and flowing natural designs on the walls and furnishings are soothing and peaceful. Decorating a room in this style is an effective way to bring the wood element into the room without it being overpowering or becoming too dominant a force.

Bring the qualities of variety, flexibility and abundance into your home with any of the following:

■ Intricately carved wooden ornaments or architectural objects.

■ Woven bamboo roof panels for a garden room.

■ Curved cane tables and chairs.

■ A bunch of straight canes tied with a coir rope.

■ Hand-made paper lampshades.

■ Split cane blinds.

■ Woven raffia baskets.

■ Banana leaf plates (these can rest on top of wooden platters).

Different plants reflect the various qualities of wood. Use them depending on which quality you want to encourage in your life:

■ Bamboo for lightness with strength.

■ Yucca for dynamic growth and new challenges

■ Palms for creating a peaceful environment.

■ Acers to encourage lightness of being.

■ Geraniums for balance and harmony.

■ Bonsai trees: for adaptability and focus.

■ Ferns for rapid growth.

■ Orchids for synthesis and an appreciation of beauty.

Plants

While wood remains a living and breathing material, living plants really bring the physicality of the wood element to life.

Our homes should nurture human relationships with nature so we can once again feel part of the natural world and find our place in it. Tending and caring for plants helps you to develop your sensitivity to beauty and increases your awareness to the more subtle environment in your home.

Plants of different shapes and colors convey different qualities. Tall upright shrubs and plants represent strength and embody the unifying properties of wood, while bushy plants with soft leaves and coloring will bring a feeling of light-heartedness to your home.

Choose a plant carefully for the conditions and position which will suit it best. Many indoor plants grow naturally in protected positions in the shade and so direct sunlight will burn their leaves. These plants are very useful in rooms which don't get much light, but take care not to block out more light by placing large plants in front of the windows. Tropical plants flourish in warmer countries and this makes them suitable for growing inside centrally-heated homes or conservatories. Remember that the air inside the home is often too dry, so they will need regular watering with a spray mist.

THE STRENGTH AND RICHNESS OF THIS WOODEN FLOOR IS COUNTERBALANCED BY THE MOVEMENT AND LIGHTNESS OF THE LARGE PAPER LANTERN HANGING FROM THE CEILING. WOOD HELPS US SEEK CHALLENGES AND PUSHES US TO THE LIMITS WHEN WE MIGHT OTHERWISE BE FEELING NERVOUS OR OVERWHELMED BY SELF-DOUBT.

Wood decoration and styles

Nature has always provided us with inspiration for themes in home decorating. In early times, homes afforded protection from the elements, but were sparsely furnished and decorated. The wood element was contained in the building structure itself and it was only used for essential pieces of furniture and functional items. As life got easier we began to use wood to beautify our homes. The longer we spend indoors the more we strive to bring nature into our homes and so over the years we have filled our homes with representations of unfurling leaves and flowers.

In the great civilizations of Islam, where representation of the human form was forbidden, leaf and plant forms are profuse. These cultures developed in hot dry places that were mostly devoid of trees. This made the wood element very special and desirable. In the great mosques, palaces and other buildings, the cool tiles and mosaics were often covered with plant life in a manmade sacred garden.

In ancient Egypt, the lotus flower was a favorite motif, while in neighboring Assyria and Babylonia the most famous pattern was that known as *hom* or the Tree of Life. As a slender stem or rugged tree, it has reappeared through the centuries. Eastern cultures have always favored natural forms for their decorative inspiration. In Japan, cherry blossom was among the most popular designs, while the Chinese often depicted blossoming trees, bamboo, flowers, and other natural forms on their furniture, pottery, wallpapers, and decorative objects.

In Britain, during the Tudor period wood was used for wall paneling and ceilings, and heavy wood furniture filled the home. Later, in Georgian times, the wood element developed into a more slender, elegant form. Decoration became light and airy, and furniture design emphasized natural symmetry and proportion.

Like seasonal cycles, there have been phases in history which have seen movements away from the harshness and coldness of modernism. Among the earlier nature revivalists were John Ruskin (1819–1900) and William Morris (1834–1896). Both these men in their own way sought to return to the simpler, more direct methods of design away from mass production. Morris was one of the main protagonists of the Arts and Crafts movement which advocated a return to nature for inspiration. The Greek acanthus leaf had been a dominant decoration on ornaments for centuries, but there was now a belief that lasting designs should be developed from other plant forms, too. Although the Arts and Crafts movement was short lived, William Morris's furniture, fabric, and wallpaper designs retain their popularity and blend well into modern homes.

In France at the turn of the nineteenth century, the Art Nouveau movement mirrored William Morris's love of natural forms. Artists and craftsmen created decorative forms which incorporated twisted branches, stems, and vines as well as stylized flowers which evolved into a very distinct style. Natural forms were featured in buildings themselves, as well as furniture, furnishings, and decorative objects.

One of the main benefits of bringing the wood element into your decorating style is that it will help to connect you to nature. The most direct way to introduce wood forms into an interior is by using them as decorating motifs in architectural details. Plasterwork and moldings often incorporate leaf and plant shapes and these can be installed into rooms of a suitable period and style. Decorative friezes, borders, and stencils can be added to rooms very quickly. Wood makes the perfect material for carving into these organic forms.

Alternative methods are to paint wood symbols onto tiles, fabrics, and wallpapers. The invention of wallpaper was a very fortunate occurrence since it provided the means for the less wealthy to enrich their walls at little cost. Originally wallpaper was handpainted and later wood-block printing and silk screen techniques allowed patterns to be

THE STRONG DESIGN OF THIS WOODEN ROOF AND THE SIMPLICITY OF THE FURNISHINGS GIVE THIS SPACE A FEELING OF CONFIDENCE AND BOLDNESS. THE ORCHID IN THE BACKGROUND INTRODUCES ANOTHER ASPECT OF THE WOOD ELEMENT, AND BRINGS CLARITY AND JUDGMENT TO THE MIND.

repeated and great quantities of wallpaper to be produced. Today wallpaper is made by both methods, and you can still find fine examples of handpainted and blocked paper.

Woodchip paper is a simple way to bring the wood element in to your home and was at one time very fashionable in itself. You can still incorporate woodchip into many of today's decorating styles, especially in a room with a Japanese or Far Eastern theme. In more traditional homes you can paint this lining paper in natural tones to enhance the wood element.

Textiles and decorative weavings will also increase the wood element in your home, as wall-hangings, door curtains, tablecloths, or furniture drapes. You could even frame them like paintings and hang them on the wall.

Paper

Perhaps the most common form of wood is paper. There are very few homes where there is not an incredible amount of paper. Books, newspapers, magazines, different types of stationery, packets, and packaging all fill our homes every day.

While books bring warmth and richness to your life, other forms of paper can easily accumulate and become clutter. If we are to honor the five elements in our homes, we need to respect them too and use them with discretion. If you have a great deal of paper cluttering up your home, it is a good idea to bundle the different types together. Take your old newspapers and cardboard to your local recycling centers, and remember that unwanted books and magazines are usually welcomed by hospitals and schools.

Here are some ideas for making the most of the richness of wood energy in books:

■ Arrange books informally on low coffee tables or ottomans.

■ Revolving bookcases are a useful way to store books when space is limited.

■ Arrange books alphabetically, by subject, by author, by height, or by theme and type.

■ Invest in a set of library steps if you need to reach books stored at high levels.

■ Keep your most precious books behind glass in a special display unit

■ Make a striking and colorful display of original paperbacks. (Penguin books used to be color coded: orange for novels, green for crime, and blue for biography.)

Books

Books are surely among the most alluring objects which fill the home. It is through the means of books that we can enjoy the quality of the wood element that promotes our own personal development and growth.

Shelves of much-loved books embody your interests, personality, and history. They exude a feeling of warmth, color, and creativity and can become an important part of a room's furnishings. In general we own far more books now than we have ever done and yet we often pay little attention to housing and displaying these to full effect. Books are best displayed in custom-built shelves and most people prefer them to be in one place rather than scattered in every room.

Like all wood products, books need to be cared for and protected if they are to last and give you pleasure. They should be kept out of direct sunlight in a well-ventilated room. Books are heavy, so shelves need to be sturdy or they will droop in the middle. You should not try to pack them in too tightly and older books need to be protected in their original jackets. Make sure you have a special place to read which incorporates a good reading lamp.

THIS CLASSICALLY DESIGNED BOOKCASE MIMICS THE LINES OF TALL TREES AND CONTAINS A FOREST OF BOOKS. SUCH AN ENVIRONMENT ENCOURAGES RELAXATION AND IS THE PERFECT PLACE TO FEAST ON THE KNOWLEDGE CONTAINED IN THE BOOKS. THE PRESENCE OF A WINGED ANGEL PROVIDES PROTECTION.

Wood lighting

We should not forget that the wood element also carries a delicacy and lightness of spirit. Paper whispers and rustles just as leaves do, and wood products talk to us in the same way. A paper lampshade hanging in a hallway or staircase can create a special and happy atmosphere. Parchment and handmade paper can be made into wonderfully textured lampshades, giving softness and intimacy to a room. In the East, paper lanterns have been used in religious festivals and celebrations for centuries. Brightly colored lanterns are carried through the streets and hung inside and outside the home. We can also enjoy this warming glow by hanging paper lanterns around our homes and gardens on special occasions.

In the creative cycle of the five elements, wood feeds fire. So a wood-burning fire will not only enhance the wood element in your home, but the fire element too. On a smaller scale, a wooden candlestick will work in harmony with the fire element of the candle.

Wood fabrics

With the exception of silk and wool, most natural fabrics contain the wood element because they are derived from plant fibers. They are an abundant and renewable source, and therefore embody the idea of variety and diversity carried by wood energy.

Cotton, jute, linen, kapok, and hemp are all useful materials in the home that can be used not only for their appearance but also for their insulating properties. Cotton and linen can be colored and printed in thousands of different ways, and are the most versatile of materials. These fabrics show the true diversity of the wood element and are excellent for drapes and furnishing fabrics in every room.

The soft silky fibers of kapok make it an excellent material for filling bedding such as mattresses and quilts. Jute has a coarse fiber which is most often woven into hessian. This can be used for wall-coverings but most frequently is made into a backing for Linoleum sheets and tiles.

Wood colors

Green represents wood and is the underlying color of nature. It is the color of expansion and regeneration, so it will help to accelerate your personal growth. Green is found at the center of the color spectrum and so it contains equal proportions of yin and yang, making it a very harmonious and balancing force. When looking at the color green the muscles in the eye can rest (the receptor rods which pick up this color are located in the center of the retina). This makes the color green extremely restful to look at and thereby healing to the body and mind.

The more yellow the green, the more it contains the energy of movement and growth. Use lime and other lighter spring greens to attract new young energy into your life. Darker greens contain the qualities of strength and the stamina of a mature tree and would be more suitable where you needed to enhance your ability to persevere and see a project through to completion. This is also a helpful color when you need inner strength to carry you through difficult times.

THESE UNUSUAL PAPER LAMPS CREATE A STYLISH AND MAGICAL CORNER IN A ROOM. THE CRINKLED EFFECT IN THEIR DESIGN MIMICS THE OVERLAPPING OF LEAVES ON A TREE, AND THE LAMPS ARE AS MUCH A WORK OF ART AS A PRACTICAL LIGHT SOURCE.

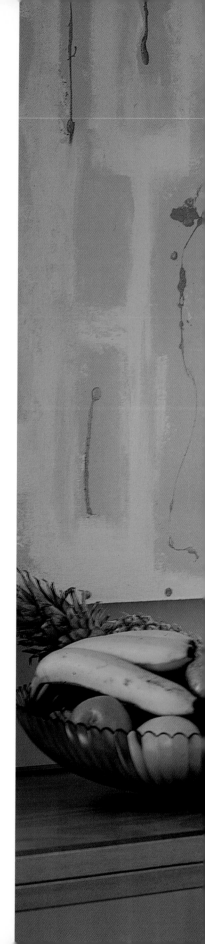

The wood home in feng shui

The Chinese were quick to honor the contribution that trees make to our lives. Around the home trees have always afforded protection from the weather and privacy from neighbors. They also have useful soundproofing qualities and bring a freshness to the air.

Wood is linked to the compass direction of east. Because this is where the sun rises each day, the wood energy also rises from this starting position. The direction your home faces therefore has significance for if your home is east-facing, this will signify a place of great wisdom and experience. The strong wood energy in your home will pass on this experience and wisdom to those who live there. This home is a teacher, communicator, and explorer. It encourages you to study and pursue knowledge and then pass on what you have learned to others.

A northeast-facing house will also be enriched with the wood qualities of wealth and possessions. This doesn't only mean material wealth, but also spiritual wealth. This house will teach you that wealth of compassion and love are greater than monetary wealth.

A southeast-facing house is known in Chinese as *An Lu*, which means health and peace. In this house you have the opportunity to enjoy good health, and there will be a good supply of creative energy found in wood and fire. You need to enhance this power with plenty of houseplants and herbs. Also, make sure you enjoy the color of spring bulbs and summer flowers.

If your home does not face east, you can still enjoy the benefits of wood energy by placing an object which represents wood in the east side of a room. This feng shui cure is believed to enhance your fame and reputation.

FIRE

FIRE

Physical attributes: muscular strength, stamina, resilience, perseverance, movement
Mental attributes: communication, action, charisma, inspiration
Compass direction: east
Home power center: living room, fireplace, and hearth

The spirit of fire

Fire is a divine energy, which can purify and inspire. It brings with it spiritual revelation and the masculine active element symbolizing both creative and destructive power. In alchemy, fire was represented graphically by the unifying symbol of a triangle.

The spirit of fire is an extremely powerful force which has always held a fascination. In fact, the ethereal properties of dynamic movement from this force, which is so difficult to contain, has a mesmerizing quality. In a very short time, fire can transform solid matter to mere ashes, and yet despite this destruction it is a highly creative force.

In the natural world, fire is the force which brings change and transformation. In some parts of the world, plant and animal life is dependent on fire destroying the environment in order for new life to take shape. This close symbolic link to birth and death has led the element of fire to play an important role in mythology and spiritual traditions all over the world. For many ancient people, the sun was the ultimate source of life and so they worshipped it as a god. Many beliefs about the formation of the world involve the creative force of fire and the gods from many cultures wheeled their power through their relationship and use of fire. The resurrection symbolism of the fire can be found in the mythical phoenix and salamander which rise again from the ashes, as does the Native American thunderbird which brings life-giving rain after the destruction of a forest or a home by a single thunderbolt.

In Christian mysticism, too, there is strong fire symbolism. Not only is fire associated with hell, it is linked to the spirit and divine will. The six-winged seraphim are always depicted as red (the fire color) and are the highest order of angels. Other angels have a close association with fire in that they played the role of great warriors and protectors. The power of fire comes from the capacity to liberate heat and light and to realize joy and fulfilment. The idea of angels having wings supports the symbolic depiction of a force which can lift your spirit closer to God.

Fire homes

One of the most outstanding qualities of fire is that it is constantly moving and changing. Fire homes, too, always seem to be in a constant state of flux. Fire people love to move furniture, decorate, and change displays and objects around their homes. Surprisingly, this does not detract from the harmony a fire home can give you.

In humankind, fire is linked to the spirit. After all we are solar beings, living in the solar system and essentially made up from solar energy. We can consider our soul as being our own internal sun, which radiates from our center, giving us a feeling of well-being. Connecting to the fire element in our homes can therefore benefit us all, regardless of our elemental personality.

THE STRONG METAL ELEMENT IN THIS SITTING ROOM IS ENRICHED BY THE SUN-BURST MIRROR WHICH ADDS SOME WARMTH, DRAMA, AND PASSION TO AN OTHERWISE SUBDUED AND QUIET ROOM.

Homes which reflect the fire element have a vibrancy and drama of their own. They may have dramatic shapes and features and they may be full of hidden surprises. The fire home is exhilarating and full of contrasting visual stimuli. There may be a variety of colors, textures, scents, and shapes.

Fire homes are confident and exhilarating places to be. They are places where you live for the moment, and so it is unlikely that you will find family heirlooms or loads of old clutter. Often the fire home is full of electrical and electronic equipment, which has its own type of energizing vibrations.

Fire energy comes to the fore in mid-summer when we are most active. I have lived in both the southern and northern hemispheres, and so I know that, on both sides of the world, the alignment of a house to the sun is one of the most important considerations for comfortable living. In the northern countries, homes facing south and southwest are the most desirable, making use of the natural warmth of the sun for as many hours of the day as possible. In the southern climates homeowners seek out the opposite alignment, for a home facing north or northeast will afford protection during the baking hot afternoons.

South-facing homes are therefore naturally blessed with an abundance of the fire element, but so are homes which radiate an inner warmth. In feng shui, south-facing homes have plenty of yang energy which is associated with the masculine principle which is physically active.

If your home has large windows which allow natural light to flood into the rooms, you will have plenty of fire power. Although many homes are warmed by central heating, this does not mean that they have a good supply of the fire element. Only rooms which have a working fireplace will be injected with the energy from this element, as will those with heating or cooking facilities which are fueled by wood or coal. The importance lies in the natural flame.

Like the curls of smoke and dancing flames, fire energy is also typified by movement and upward spirals. The staircase is the perfect place for energy to rise up through the house and energize the upper floors. The staircase can be thought of as the backbone of a house, the treads like vertebrae that give the home vitality and strength. Houses with spiral staircases, or those which have a stairs which circle upwards in the stairwell will help the occupants to develop a strength of character and help them stick to their convictions.

Bringing the fire element into the home

It is through the element of fire that a home is enlivened and comes to life. Without the fire element, it remains cold and detached and somewhere more suited to house machines than human beings.

The close link between the fire element and light makes its presence in many forms indispensable in the home. Not only should your home have as much natural light from the sun as possible, it also needs to generate its own light and energy. To do this you need the fire element. Fire creates living light, which is quite different from that generated by electricity.

Firelight is special because, like the summer, it is dynamic, vibrant, and expansive. As water determines our longevity, fire determines our breadth and scope. The fire element helps you make a home which is energizing and stimulating. This doesn't mean that you will want to move about in it all the time, but that you will be enthusiastic in all that you do.

The transformative powers of light can help you change aspects of your home and your life for the better, into a whole new world. For this reason, when you move into a new home, it is best to activate the fire element as soon as you arrive. We symbolically need to burn out the old and welcome in the new. If you have several projects which need to be undertaken in your new house, make sure that checking or installing a fireplace and hearth is the first that you attend to. When you arrive in your new home, light a candle and take it into every room. This has the same effect as turning on your elemental light switch. The fire element will generate lightness and warmth into your whole house.

As the staircase provides a means of communication between different floors, it is a good place to energize with fire energy. Paint your entrance hall and stairwell with rich red fire colors, and make sure that they are well lit. If you have a modern home, install sparkling footlights to light your way upstairs, or insert mirror mosaics into the plasterwork alongside the staircase. A pendulum clock in the entrance hall will also stimulate fire energy to rise up the stairs. Alternatively you could hang rich banners or paintings up the staircase.

Your home draws primary power from the fireplace and hearth which creates a direct and dynamic connection between ground and sky. This is the *hara* center of the home, the seat of power, which can be enhanced by sitting in front of living flames. The most obvious way to bring fire energy into the home is by literally burning a fire. This could be in an open fireplace or a wood-burning stove. The flames of a candle also carry the fire element and so candles are invaluable portable sun packages which can be moved around the house with ease.

Fire and light go hand in hand, and so do fire and warmth. The fire element brings not only physical warmth but emotional warmth into your home. We naturally gravitate toward living flames and the hearth is the place that you are most likely to enjoy intimate exchanges and moments of sharing with your partner, family, and friends.

There is no building design or architectural style for a room which cannot be enhanced by a fireplace. Most older homes had fireplaces in many rooms, and many modern homes still have the hearth as a room's central focus. Unfortunately some builders and designers do not appreciate the energetic importance of the fireplace and many houses are now being built without this important feature. Although we can easily heat a home with central heating, building a house without a fireplace is like a person being born without a heart. A television screen as the central focus in your living room is a poor substitute for a fire as this will diminish your energy rather than increasing your vitality.

If there is no fireplace in your main living area, it is not difficult to install a living flame gas fire and surround it with a mantel. Many multi-fuel stoves are energy efficient and perfect for a modern home. The hearth can be made from granite, stone, or marble and an overmantel fashioned from wood or metal. The fire element in your living room will create an environment where you will feel able to establish a vision of yourself through creativity and self-expression.

If you don't have a fireplace and prefer not to install one, you can create a power center using colors and shapes which represent the sun. Make a focal point on a shelf, table, or floor on which you can arrange objects which suggest fire. A bright yellow candle, or a bowl of sunflowers can radiate this positive force and boost your self-esteem. Objects made from gold or brass, or painted gold are good for involving the fire element. If you can, find a chunk of citrine or pyrite, also known as "fool's gold" because this mineral carries a strong fire energy.

You can enhance the fire element in other ways too. As wood fuels fire, the presence of wood in the home will support the effects of fire. Red-colored woods, such as mahogany, cedar, teak, and redwood are the best types to use in a fire home. These should be highly polished. Interestingly, there are some metals which have more of an affinity with the fire element than others. These include those with a yellow hue, such as copper and gold, or iron, which is linked to the fiery planet Mars. Other highly polished metals such as aluminum and stainless steel also

Warm-colored and opalescent gems and metals reflect the fire element and represent different qualities:

■ Gold, copper, and brass represent high ideals.

■ Opal represents having many talents.

■ Ruby and garnet represent love and passion.

■ Bloodstone represents spiritual strength.

■ Tiger's eye represents inner strength.

■ Citrine represents transformation.

■ Aluminum and stainless steel represent communication.

have the reflective qualities of fire, especially when placed near warm fiery colors.

Traditionally the fire element has strong associations with the kitchen, as the main fireplace was located here and so became the center of the home. With the trend in open-plan living, the fire element can be beneficial to both your cooking and living areas. If your kitchen is a separate room, you can still introduce a strong fire element where it will enhance your creativity and communication skills. However, it may also become a hot and uncomfortable place to be for any length of time. It is better therefore to use the wood element in the kitchen. Wood fuels fire in the creative cycle and so the fire element will be enhanced without being overpowering.

Although unsuitable for most bedrooms, the presence of the fire element in your bedroom will make it a luxurious and sensual place, where you can celebrate your sexuality. Add shiny red cushions, red candles, or sparkling beaded bed drapes for those special occasions but remember that fire is energizing and not conducive to sleep. It is best to keep the fire element out of the bathroom, as fire and water don't mix.

THE ROARING FIRE IN THIS MAGNIFICENT FIREPLACE FILLS THE LIVING ROOM WITH CHARISMA AND INTIMACY. THE DRAMATIC COLOR SCHEME COMBINES WARM AND COOLER FIRE COLORS TO CREATE A SPACE WHICH ENHANCES THE POWER OF COMMUNICATION AND SOCIABILITY.

Fire accessories

The reflective qualities of fire are present in fire accessories of all types. Fabrics are soft, sensual, and pliable and made from silks, satins, shantung, brocade, velvet, and other fabrics with a shiny surface. Silk especially has excellent saturation, giving it an intensity of color not found in other fabrics. Fire fabrics often have several colors woven into the cloth, or the fabric may have been through several dye processes. Indonesian and Javanese batik use a process of hot wax and often use strong swirling designs. In China and India embroidery frequently depicts fire symbols like dragons, peacocks, and snakes.

Other designs which show the movement and energy of fire are geometrical designs such as hound's-tooth check, zigzags and bold patterns. These may be difficult to live with as they can give out jarring energy patterns which overstimulate the mind and nervous system, so it is best to use them with restraint.

Japanese and Chinese lacquerware is another excellent fire accessory. Colored pigments, often black and red, are added to the lacquer which is highly polished. If you can find any piece of antique or modern furniture with a lacquer finish it will help to bring the fire element into your home.

Another simple way to enhance the fire element in a room is to introduce a plant or flower with fire energy. Many plants which grow in hot places are red in color, and some resemble red hot pokers or torches. Red arum lilies look like flames, while the dramatic strelitzia flower, also known as the bird of paradise, has touches of fiery red on its "head." Any fast-growing plant will contain some fire energy especially those with spiky leaves, such as the spider plant.

For a longer-lasting effect you can introduce large bold pictures into your room.

Fire colors

When you look carefully at the flames in a fire you will notice that like the fire, the flames dance and change color. The overall effect of a fire is a glowing golden orange, but when you look more closely you will see that flames also reflect other colors too. At the base of a candle flame there will often be a clear green, and as the flame gets hotter this turns into a blue. The hottest of flames actually become white hot.

Color is a wonderful way to invoke the dramatic qualities of the fire element. Any rich warm tones create a welcoming and cozy atmosphere. These are particularly appreciated in dark rooms and during the cooler winter months. You have to remember that these strong hot colors may be comforting in the depths of winter, but they could be much too heavy and uncomfortable when the weather warms up. To reflect the proportions of colors found in living flames you should compliment your warm colors with blue, green, and white. If your walls are a warm shade of red, the furnishings could be cooler in tone, and plenty of green plants will give a more balanced effect.

A good way of creating the translucent quality of fire on your walls is to build up a series of thin color glazes on top of a pale base coat. By applying several layers of washes or glazes you create a shimmering effect which will reflect light in different ways throughout the day. At night the walls will be enhanced by soft lighting or candlelight. Just a touch of vibrant fire color in a cool room can change the chemistry and atmosphere there. If a room is dark and cold, fire brings warmth and encourages a more creative and sociable environment. In predominantly wood and earth rooms, fire energy could help you to complete tasks, while adding the water element will tone down fire colors if they are overpowering.

The fire element and feng shui

The fire element is imbued with forceful masculine energy and is the element which is the most yang in Chinese philosophy. This makes it a dynamic force to get things moving and when you need to take forceful action to achieve a goal. In feng shui, the fire element can be used to instigate change and make things happen. By its nature fire is always on the move, so a house which is permanently filled with fire will not be a relaxed and peaceful place to live. This is why it is better to introduce this element in small movable objects which can be cleared away when you have achieved the desired result.

If you wish to implement the color and element relationships used in the art of feng shui, you need to use just one auspicious color. The Chinese link red to fire, and in the practice of feng shui, this color has greatest power when used in the south or southeast area of a room or house.

One of the feng shui cures for a home which needs more fire energy is that of the crystal pendant. A crystal, which can be made from either glass or perspex, is hung in a window and acts as a prism sending rainbows of light around the room. I was lucky enough to find some pendants from a crystal chandelier in an antique shop, and these high-quality cut-glass pieces throw exquisite fiery flashes into my living room.

The Chinese believe that good health and harmony depend on a good flow of Chi, the breath of life, around the home and through the body. Electrical and mechanical equipment, such as clocks, TV sets and stereos, generate movement of Chi and therefore stir up the fire element in your home. So if you find you are unable to concentrate or relax you need to check that it is not these items which are the culprits. They are however most useful in moving stagnant energy from corners of your rooms and hidden areas under stairs.

To enhance the fire element in your home you don't have to create rooms which look like a towering inferno. Fire rooms can be subtle, elegant, and sophisticated. Their natural drama often comes from one central point of focus, or a touch of hot color which stands out against a neutral cool background.

The fire element has the capacity to stimulate the senses and is traditionally linked to the fireplace. It is a source of comfort because it provides the home with a protective quality against any threat from outside. In Native American tradition, the camp fire was the image of happiness and prosperity and the sun itself was called "the great fire." When there is a fireplace in the kitchen, it is regarded as the heart of the home and a place of nurturing. This part of the home is most closely linked with nature and natural processes.

The house facing south or southeast (an lu) is an area which represents health and peace. It is a place where you should feel joyful and energetic. Even if your room is in the basement or some other dark space, natural flames from candles or an open fire will enliven the room with sparkle and vitality. The power of fire comes from its capacity to generate and liberate heat and light, so the qualities of joy and fulfilment are reflected in our lives. Even if your home does not face this direction, if you feel tired and washed out, you need to stimulate the southern side of your home. Yang energy is the best catalyst for instigating change in the home. Bright light is considered a strong, dynamic, and masculine force, and therefore extremely yang in quality. Simply pulling back drapes to allow sunlight to pour through a window into a dark room will invigorate the space.

Here are simple ways to bring the element of fire into your home:

- Arrange silk cushions diagonally on your sofa.

- Light a pyramid-shaped orange candle.

- Grow cacti and other pointed-leafed plants in a copper container.

- Introduce sunflowers to a room by hanging prints on walls or choose furnishings with a sunflower pattern.

- Hang a gold-leafed round framed mirror, preferably one that is supported by wings.

- Use a brass three-pronged candelabra with red candles.

- Install a picture or mural with a thunderbird or phoenix design.

You should use fire rituals
in the home:

■ To cleanse the
atmosphere from any type
of pollution.

■ After an illness or death.

■ When clearing out a
disused or dark room.

■ To bring more joy and
light into your life.

■ To protect your home
after a break-in.

■ To guard against harmful
outside forces.

■ To warm a cold heart.

Fire rituals

Fire is probably the most used element in rituals around the world. Fire commands respect and a feeling of awe, and its power strikes both fear and admiration in observers. Its ability to purify our environment and transform our inner being makes it perfect for use in the home. Fire can bring about inner purification too. Fire often symbolizes the union with the divine, transcendence of the human condition, and it also tests our purity and faith. Buddha is often represented as a pillar of fire, a metaphor for mystical illumination.

In many parts of the world the lighting of a bonfire still marks special events and occasions. Bonfires can symbolize the return of sunlight after winter, and in Japan, Shinto fires at New Year are intended to forestall the threat of any destructive fires in the year ahead. Fire rituals often involve the symbolic lighting of candles or the burning of incense, which cleanse and purify the atmosphere and afford protection to the home. So burning a candle or incense is an easy way to energize the fire energy. Similarly, just sitting by an open fire is a very therapeutic activity; the fire holds your attention while it purifies your negative thoughts and emotions.

Different sounds and types of music carry different patterns of energy, so using sound is one of the best ways to enhance the qualities of the natural elements. The simplest and most effective way of instilling fire energy with sound is by clapping. Walk round the room while clapping your hands, especially in the corners. If you have a drum or rattle, a steady beat is also very effective.

Fire music is loud, vibrant, and dynamic. It really makes you want to move. Drumming, which was often performed around a camp fire in ancient rites and rituals, is excellent fire music, but you can play any favorite music that has a strong beat and base rhythm.

Instilling fire energy through chanting

Chanting is another excellent way of instilling fire energy into your home. The power of the chant is in the energy created by your voice through the repetition of words, rather like drumming. You will be able to feel an energizing effect inside you. First, you need to build up the power of your chant. Keep chanting for several minutes until you feel compelled to move. Then walk through the house chanting as you go. I use the chant, *Fire my home, fire enthrone, fire excite, fire unite.*

A ritual to exorcise negative forces

Every color has its negative side, and red is also the color of anger, danger, and poison. This could be anything poisonous to your well-being including a poison tongue or thoughts.

This Navaho prayer was used to exorcise evil by moving it into a mythical place where it is destroyed. Light a red candle before you invoke it. The candle should be lit on four bright and four dark nights over a period of time. The light and dark nights can occur in any order, as long as you light the candle eight times. Repeat the prayer each time you light the candle.

Away behind the first muddy red river
Away behind the second muddy red river
Away behind the third muddy red river
Away behind the fourth muddy red river

Away behind the first red rock
Away behind the second red rock
Away behind the third red rock
Away behind the fourth red rock

ANOTHER WAY TO MOVE STAGNANT ENERGY AND CHANGE
THE ATMOSPHERE IN A ROOM IS BY ADOPTING THE
ASYMMETRICAL ARRANGEMENT OF SHAPES. HERE THE
FORCE OF FIRE IS MAGNIFIED BY AN ANGULAR LAMP STAND.

An energizing ritual using the color red

This ritual uses creative visualization to move the energy around your home or a single room. You can, however, also perform this ritual by walking around the space. Ideally you should sit in the south or southeast side of your home and have a red object in front of you on which to focus. Close your eyes and make sure you have a strong connection with the ground through your feet. Imagine red energy coming from deep within the earth and rising up through your feet into the base of your spine. You should feel this area getting warm and tingling. Allow the fire energy to rise up through your spine and travel down your arms to your fingertips. Imagine you are walking through each room of your house starting at the front door, or if you are energizing one room, move around this room starting at the door. As you walk push fire energy into the room. You can also instill this energy into different objects by touching them. As you do this, you will feel the room getting warmer and the objects that you touch will seem to glow. Move around the space until you are satisfied that it is sufficiently energized.

EARTH

EARTH

Physical attributes: stabilizing, inertia, synthesizing
Mental attributes: pacifying, calming, receptivity
Compass direction: center
Home power center: kitchen

The spirit of earth

The earth is the universal symbol of maternal protection and sustenance. It is not surprising therefore that most creation myths embody the theory that the first humans were formed from mud, clay, or even sand. The mother goddess, such as the classical Gaia, was seen to be the source of all life.

In China the earth is represented by a square, because this geometric figure is extremely stable. However, other cultures link the earth to a circle, which is more in keeping with the idea of a womb and an enclosed protective space.

The spirit of earth helps us find a point of balance in our lives so that we can develop a greater perception and perspective on life. Before undertaking a course of action, we need to center ourselves. This brings together and unifies all the physical and mental energy we need to undertake a task. The earth element helps us integrate different aspects of our life, and helps us to appreciate the importance of paying equal amounts of attention to our physical, mental, and spiritual needs.

Earth energy moves in circles which link us to the circle of life. Each point on the circle is of equal value, and this understanding allows us to experience the significance of the present. By tuning in to the earth element we can enjoy and find meaning in every moment and so put life into context.

Earth interiors

Some homes have a natural feeling of safety and stability, and you will know that these places have a powerful earth energy. You can usually feel the warm and welcoming atmosphere as soon as you enter, and you will get the feeling that you are "coming home" even if the house doesn't belong to you.

The earth home has an organic feeling to it, as if it has evolved over a long period of time. This may be reflected in an eclectic mixture of furniture and furnishings. Some of these may have been collected by you on your travels while other items may have been passed down through the family. Earth homes are tactile places where you are tempted to pick up objects and feel and smell them. Rich sweet aromas play a role in the earthy home as do color and taste.

The interior of an earth home is one which stimulates all the senses. It may have earthy colors, rich textures, and aromas. The living area is likely to have large overstuffed sofas and comfortable chairs. Beanbags, rounded footstools and other rounded forms all go to making the earth home a place that you can literally sink into. There are also likely to be interesting and varied natural woven textiles on chairs, walls, and floors. The keynote, however, is softness and so fabrics and materials such as suede or velvet will have a rich pile.

The kitchen is the center of the earth home, as this is the place where we nourish ourselves and our family. The earthy kitchen is filled with natural materials, rough wooden utensils, and hand-thrown pottery. On the window sills there are aromatic herbs in ceramic pots, and ideally there should be a rich warm aroma, such as newly baked bread or freshly ground coffee.

Decorating styles which convey earth qualities include the rich warm and bright colors and shapes found in Mexico. Terracotta pots and tiles, as well as ceramic artifacts and wall plaques, convey the strong earth connection of the people who live in this hot and vibrant country.

Another earthy style is found in the Mediterranean especially in Spain and Italy. The Spanish hacienda and traditional finca blend well into the natural landscape. Such houses are planned with a central courtyard, a place of protection at their heart. The walls are thick and solid and the roofs are usually covered with ceramic glazed tiles. In this type of building, it is quite common to find large domed spaces, plenty of rounded archways, and large molded fireplaces, bread or pizza ovens.

My Italian cousins live in a converted stone barn, where one of the inner walls is the natural rock face of the hill on which the barn was built. In this home and on its terrace there are five different ovens. Fire supports earth in the creative cycle, so this house has very powerful energy.

In Mediterranean-style homes, furniture is large and heavy, and objects tend to remain in one place for a good length of time. There is also a wealth of hand-baked tiles on floor and walls, together with decorative and useful ceramic urns and pots. Many of these structures incorporate a central water feature, which acts as a balance to control the strong earth element.

It is perhaps in Africa that the purest earth homes are found. Like many people who live close to the earth, Africans traditionally built their homes out of baked mud and made them circular in shape. African artifacts, animal skins, baskets, beadwork, pottery, and decorative items can enhance the earth connection in any home.

If you need to enhance the earth energy you do not have to follow a specific style, as there are other ways of bringing this grounding energy into your home.

Times to enhance the earth element:

■ If you have an earth personality.

■ If you live in a predominantly water home.

■ If you move house often.

■ When you wish to nurture a more stable and harmonious relationship.

■ When you need to slow down.

■ When you move house and wish to put down firm foundations.

■ When you need to remember who you are and where you belong.

THESE GLOWING HANDMADE TERRACOTTA TILES IMPROVE THE NURTURING QUALITY OF THE EARTH ELEMENT. THE COLOR VARIATIONS AND DIFFERENT SHADES IN THE TILES HELP US TO REMEMBER THAT THE EARTH IS ALIVE.

Ways to enhance the earth
element in the kitchen:

■ Eat off round handmade
pottery plates and bowls.

■ Use squat fat-bellied
jugs and storage
containers.

■ Display and eat plenty of
ground crops including
pulses and beans.

■ Use rich colored earth
pigments on the walls.

■ Lay terracotta or stone
floor tiles.

■ Prepare ground herbs
and spices in a stone
mortar and pestle.

■ Make a display of
summer or winter squashes
in a large bowl.

■ Feast your eyes on
sweet and aromatic orange
and yellow spices in jars.
Include nutmeg, mace,
turmeric, coriander,
cinnamon sticks, and
vanilla pods.

Enhancing the earth element in the home

The earth element is closely connected to the stomach so earthenware objects can be used to great effect in the kitchen where they reinforce the nurturing properties of this element. Ceramics are warm to the touch and are comforting to handle. Choose bowls, vases, and containers which have full, rounded forms echoing the image of the mother earth. The curves of earth objects give them the appearance of stability and weight so that they are unlikely to fall over, a quality which can be transferred to us. Objects made of clay give us a feeling of security and literally bring us down to earth. Squat milk jugs and brown glazed pots are perfect for conveying this feeling.

Glazed tiles and ceramics are durable materials, which are useful in areas of the home where they will get wet. Traditional hand-painted tiles can be found in a range of natural colors from red, brown, and ocher through to green and blue, while glazes are made from rocks and minerals, allowing these elements to work hand in hand.

Paints can also be made from ground earth, and those made from natural pigments provide a healthy and environmentally friendly atmosphere in the home. With most of us spending so much of our time inside, a healthy indoor atmosphere, free of poisonous emissions and long-term untested synthetics, is of paramount importance to reestablish strong immune systems which help our resistance to disease. Earth and mineral pigments are also ideal for allergy sufferers and in homes occupied by the very young and the elderly.

Earth is linked to the summer season, with its clear days and variety of rich, strong colors. When you need to bring some summer sunshine into rooms where other elements predominate, a range of earthy colors such as ocher, sienna, ultramarine, umber, pink, cream, soft and clear green will enhance the feel-good factor. Colors made from earth pigments are in harmony with our own natural coloring so that we find them easy to live with. Their warm loving vibrations encourage a spirit of sociability and community.

Food carries elemental qualities, and is an immediate way of introducing specific health qualities into your system. Shaman healer and author Denise Linn in her book *Feng Shui for the Soul* describes food like this. "Honoring the food you bring into the home is one of the most powerful ways to activate the forces of the earth in your environment." Food contains not only physical nutrients but energetic ones too. This vibrational energy feeds our energy system through the chakras which are subtle connection points sited along the spine.

Many earthy foods grow underground, and are fully of minerals and nutrients. Vegetables and seeds carry a strong earth energy, especially when they are round in shape, of rich gold, orange, or brown coloring and growing low to the ground. The late summer is the time when fruit and vegetables ripen naturally in the sun. This brings out their innate sweetness and also gives them time to soak up the energy from the earth. Summer pumpkins and squashes are perfect earth foods, and you can hollow and dry their shells to make attractive objects that will adorn your home, while enhancing the earth element.

MEDITERRANEAN STYLE CAPTURES EARTH QUALITIES
PARTICULARLY WELL. THE RICH ORANGE WALLS COCOON
THIS BEDROOM IN COMFORTING WARMTH AND SECURITY.

Earth lighting

Imagine the light of the late afternoon sun on a warm sunny day. Everything takes on a soft and golden glow. This type of reflected warm light creates a feeling of relaxation and warmth in us too. We can introduce a similar type of lighting into our home, to re-create this comforting feeling.

Reflect light from lamps off warm-colored walls, or wash a glazed wall with a spotlight. Ceramic lamps with rounded squat bases with warm-colored glass shades will create an intimate and relaxed atmosphere. Red, orange, and yellow candles placed in sand or earthenware pots create the perfect convivial atmosphere when placed on a coffee or dining table. These colors induce sociability and promote conversation and a sharing of feelings.

COMBINING DIFFERENT TYPES OF LIGHTING IN ONE ROOM GIVES YOU THE OPPORTUNITY TO CREATE MANY MOODS. IN COOLER CLIMATES THE WARMTH OF THE SUN CAN BE ENHANCED DURING THE DAY WITH YELLOW-COLORED WALLS, WHICH ALSO INTENSIFY THE EFFECTIVENESS OF ARTIFICAL LIIGHT AT NIGHT.

Establishing your earth connection

In Chinese philosophy the earth itself has an equal balance of yin and yang energy, and this is why it provides a perfect home to all life on earth. The type of environment in which we live is largely dependent on the type of energy in the earth in that place. So the earth creates a central focus around which our lives can revolve.

Unfortunately we have lost our sensitivity to the earth and our respect for it. Not only do we spend most of our lives indoors, we are also using fewer materials made from the earth in our homes. Baked clay bricks are rapidly being replaced by concrete blocks, steel, or timber products. Inside the home too, mud floors, earthenware bricks, or tiles are being replaced with synthetic carpet and vinyl. Many people live above ground in apartments and tower blocks. If you are one of these people you will find it more difficult to put down roots and maintain a stable lifestyle. Living high above the ground affects one's ability to form long-lasting bonds and you are more likely to be less practical and down to earth than if you were living at ground level.

Not only have we separated ourselves from the earth, but we have reinforced this by continually wearing shoes both indoors and outdoors. Parents are now discouraging children from playing in the earth outside, for fear of them getting dirt on their bodies and clothing and bringing it into the house. As a result many people grow up thinking that the earth is dirty and unpleasant and it is not surprising that so many yards today are covered in concrete or gravel.

By losing our earth connection we have lost our way and no longer respect and nourish our spiritual mother, the earth. However, our homes can provide us with a lifeline, so we can regain this essential connection. Whatever materials make up the fabric of your home, you can make a symbolic act to enhance the qualities of the earth element.

Whether you live in a bungalow or several floors up, there is one place which provides a strong connection point to the earth. This can be found at the center of your home. You can also find a power point in the middle of your yard. It is in this central position we can renew our earth connection. If your home has more than one floor, it is on the floor closest to the ground that you will find the earth power point. Here is a simple method for finding this place and renewing your earth connection.

Find the center of your home. You may have to use your intuition to find the exact location if you have an irregular shaped building. Take off your shoes so that you stand barefooted on this spot. Close your eyes and imagine a line of energy coming up from deep inside the earth. Imagine it as a wave of golden light, coming up through your feet and traveling upward through your legs and out of the top of your head. Now imagine the energy moving downward again, strengthening your earth connection. Continue focusing on this energy moving up and down, until it settles in your solar-plexus (stomach area). You should notice a feeling of contentment and happiness.

The central earth element position is a good area to place something permanently to strengthen the connection between you and your home. An earthenware bowl, an arrangement of pebbles or stones, a ceramic urn or planter, or a ceramic statue would all be suitable. If you have a basement or cellar in your house, it is a good idea is to "ground" your home there. The effect will be to make your life more stable, and bring you a feeling of permanence and security. If you are prone to moving house and do not feel like you belong anywhere, doing this will slow down the

AN ARRANGEMENT OF PEBBLES BRINGS THE FEELING OF LOYALTY, SECURITY, AND PREDICTABILITY TO YOUR HOME. HANDLE YOUR PEBBLES WHEN YOU NEED TO BECOME INVOLVED AND FEEL NEEDED. PLACING THE STONES TOGETHER IN A GROUP SYMBOLIZES TOGETHERNESS.

To stimulate the earth element with color or mentally invoke the earth element in this area:

■ Place a yellow or orange toned circular rug in the center of the room.

■ Hang a ceramic bead curtain over a doorway.

■ Walk barefoot in a circle or trace a circle in the air with your hand.

■ Visualize a ball of yellow energy rising up from the earth and filling your room from the center outwards.

desire to move and help you to stay put. It will also help you manifest your ideas and dreams into physical reality.

You have to remember that sometimes placing an object in the center of a room will interfere with your movement around your home. In that case you can make the earth connection at floor level or even by painting an earth symbol on the ceiling.

Although the earth itself contains an equal proportion of yin and yang energy which renders it stable, the presence of other elements can throw this harmony out of balance. As a result our homes become less secure. This doesn't mean we should turn our homes into fortresses, but if a house gives out an impression of security and strength, it creates a psychological barrier against threats from outside. By reinforcing the protection afforded by the earth element we can ward off unwanted intruders in a very subtle way. Regular shapes have a quality of strength with no visual weak points where you can enter without alarming the householders. So the earth home can afford us not only physical but psychological protection too.

Each of us is surrounded by a magnetic field, often referred to as the aura. This creates our personal space which we naturally defend. If a stranger stands too close, you will automatically feel uncomfortable, and this is because your personal space has been invaded. So your ability to feel relaxed and comfortable depends on your psychological defence of your personal space.

Even though we are learning physically to protect our homes, we often forget to protect our immediate environment outdoors in the yard. Even if you live in an apartment or in a town house, you may have a patio area or front yard extending from the gate to the front door. There are also spaces we forget along the sides of the buildings and behind them. These are all areas you should consider when adjusting the elemental forces which may be weakening the defensive earth element in your home environment.

IN THIS BATHROOM YOU WILL FEEL PRIVATE AND PROTECTED. ITS DEEP APRICOT-COLORED WALLS WILL GIVE YOUR SKIN A WARM GLOW AND YOU WILL LEAVE THE ROOM FEELING REFRESHED, POSITIVE, AND FULL OF SELF-CONFIDENCE.

If you have not thought about your intention for your present home, you can use the earth element to discover this. You should perform rituals using the earth element:

■ To help you to remember good times and people you love.

■ To help you to discover your intention for your home.

■ To help to stabilize you if you have moved house often.

■ To give you a sense of security and belonging.

Rituals to enhance the earth element

The ritual of intention

One of the main qualities which the earth element embodies is that of intention. When we move into a new home, we unconsciously or consciously have an intention for that place. It may be that we only intend to stay there for a short time or just until we have accomplished or journeyed through a particular phase in our life. Perhaps you intend to stay in the house in order to raise a family, or it may be you intend to enjoy your retirement and wish to end your days in that place. What is extraordinary about our intentions is that they become self-fulfilling and we usually move on, once the house has satisfied these needs.

The ritual of remembering

Another quality of the earth element is that of remembering and this is one of the main reasons why this element was so important in many ancient cultures. The earth element helps you remember where you come from and where you belong. You can use it to honor the memory of your ancestors and others.

Collect some photographs or pictures of anyone who you wish to remember. Or if available, use some artifacts or objects which belonged to them or which remind you of them. You also need a red or yellow candle. Create a home altar using a piece of cloth on the floor or a low table and place it in the center of the room. Place four rocks or pebbles on the four corners of the cloth, and put your objects in the center.

Light the candle, sit quietly and look at your pictures and objects. Remember.

When you have finished, say "I honor and remember you (the person's name)" for each person that you are remembering.

Light, aroma, and sound

In China, the earth element is given a central position, around which the other four elements move. The synthesizing and balancing qualities of the earth element are therefore strongest when activated at the center of the home. Most often it is not practical to place a large piece of furniture or furnishing in the center of your house, or even in the center of a room, so it is better to instill the earth element symbolically.

This can be done in several ways using light, aroma, and sound. Each elemental force is associated with a certain taste and flavor. In the case of the earth element, a sweet taste and fragrant floral or grounding note convey these vibrations. Try burning incense or aromatherapy oils of sandalwood, cedar, bergamot, sweet orange, rose, or benzoin to establish an earth connection in a room. This will help to stabilize and ground you.

Sweet mellow sounds of the cello or oboe are perfect for creating a feel-good factor. Listening to traditional jazz, country, or blues music is especially good for people with an earth personality as the strong melodies and base rhythms are in harmony with their internal vibrations.

For people who are less practical and for those who have their heads in the air, the stronger beat of drums is perfect earth music. The drum and its rhythm harness the energy of the earth. A drumbeat also stimulates the flow of blood and adrenaline in the body, so that you become more fully awake and your self-awareness will increase. Playing earth music can help you find and focus on your path in life, so that you are fortified and able to meet life's challenges.

SURROUNDING YOURSELF WITH PICTURES OF LOVED ONES AND HAPPY TIMES HELPS YOU TO DEVELOP A STRONG SENSE OF IDENTITY AND BELONGING. THESE OBJECTS LINK TO THE EARTH ELEMENT WHICH HELPS US TO VALUE OURSELVES MORE.

METAL

METAL

Physical attributes: hard, cold, straight, pure, strong, condensed
Mental attributes: wisdom and understanding, rest and relaxation, self-reflection
Compass direction: north
Home power center: sanctuary, study, or fitness center

Different metals are linked to different planets and each has its own special qualities.

Lead is linked to Saturn contemplation, morality, and stability

Tin is linked to Jupiter power, optimism, and organization

Iron is linked to Mars masculine energy, action, and strength

Copper is linked to Venus love, imagination, and harmony

Mercury is linked to Mercury fluidity, flexibility, and transformation

Silver is linked to the Moon feminine energy, compassion, and nurturing

Gold is linked to the Sun joy and power with wisdom

The spirit of metal

Metal is a magical element for through its energy it helps to create perfection of form and function. The dense energy of metal is found in all rocks, minerals, and gemstones and we can see this in the hardness, coldness, and sharpness of the forms it creates. In order to produce metal, minerals undergo great transmutation through heat and pressure. This happens whether metal is being formed through natural processes or through human manufacture.

Although the densest of all materials known to us, metals are made of cosmic energy trapped in physical form, and like all earthly living creatures have celestial potential. This is why the spirit of metal and its relationship to the planets and the earth is so attractive to us. The movement of energy through metal is inward, giving metal the power to bring focus and concentration to our minds. In the home you can introduce different types of metal to enhance the qualities to which they are linked.

Most metals are found in a place of darkness deep within the earth and are created over millions of years in an endless cycle of heating and cooling within the core of the earth. As metal contracts and hardens when it cools, it mimics the season of autumn which is nature's time of decline and gathering in. Metal is cold to the touch, so it is linked to the color white which also conveys a sense of coolness and clarity of purpose.

Those who work with the metal element become masters of ceremony and discipline. It is the one element which is typified by detachment from the senses, and it promotes a serenity which comes from aesthetic and high moral values. The metal element will help you to cultivate an eye for beauty of form and line.

The metal interior

The metal interior, like the metal personality, is cool, calm, and collected. When you enter a metal home, your emotions are depressed and you feel a quiet detachment. Metal rooms are minimal and uncluttered. If the building has a metal structure, its ceilings will often be high and the rooms will be large, airy, and bright. Each piece of furniture, picture, and decorative object appears to have been deliberately chosen and each thing feels special. The atmosphere is unhurried and you are likely to feel that you could spend time quietly contemplating the space.

Metal interiors lack fussiness and softness. The furniture and fittings are often made of metal and glass, or other cold and hard materials. The metal interior is not an emotionally comforting and relaxing place, as the energy is much more connected to the mind. So your enjoyment comes from intellectual appreciation of the forms and beauty of the objects around you. Even if you are not an art collector, a metal home is a tidy and orderly environment where everything has a place. This creates a sense of comfort and familiarity.

THIS COOL AND SIMPLE INTERIOR REFLECTS A STRONG METAL ELEMENT, WHICH HELPS US TO STAY CALM AND CENTERED. THIS IS A GOOD INTERIOR FOR BUSY, DISORGANIZED PEOPLE AS IT PROVIDES A SENSE OF FOCUS AND QUIET DETACHMENT.

Using metal in the home

Throughout history we have measured the advancement of civilizations by their ability to extract and manufacture tools from metals. The density of the atoms of most metals creates a material of great hardness enabling us to fashion items which are light in appearance but great in strength. It is little wonder therefore that metal is used widely as a building material and many objects in the home are fashioned from this attractive and durable material.

Unfortunately, the wide availability of metal has meant that we frequently tend to forget that minerals are a non-renewable and precious resource. Some metals are still abundant, but we are fast depleting the earth's supply of other metals such as lead, tin, and zinc. It is essential, therefore, that whenever possible we should recycle this dwindling resource and honor this element with restraint and respect.

Although metals have greatly enhanced our lives, they can also be poisonous to us. So it is important that we use this element in the home with care. Some metals give off toxic vapors when concentrated in the home, especially as they are included in many types of paints and solvents. The predominance of metal in a building can be hazardous too, and structures made of large steel beams can interfere with the earth's electro-magnetic field. This interference affects the balance of ions in the air and the resulting disturbed energy fields have been found to cause and exacerbate some serious diseases.

Few people find a metal home environment comfortable, and it is only those who feel they would like a truly minimal lifestyle that should

A BOWL OF RED AND ORANGE FOOD (FIRE) CONTROLS THE POWERFUL METAL ELEMENT IN THIS KITCHEN WHICH WOULD OTHERWISE CREATE A CYNICAL AND RETICENT STATE OF MIND.

You can create a peaceful and quiet space energized with metal with the addition of any of the following:

- ▪ A white leather sofa.

- ▪ A light wood table with metal legs.

- ▪ A nest of perspex tables.

- ▪ An arum lily in a metal pot.

- ▪ An aluminum standing lamp focusing light on a wall.

- ▪ A curved metal screen.

- ▪ A door covered with metal sheets or metal studs.

To reap the full benefit of the metal element in a home gym you will need:

- ▪ Silver or white venetian or roller blinds.

- ▪ A floor-to-ceiling mirror.

- ▪ Good low-halogen recessed lighting.

- ▪ A silver coloured clock.

- ▪ Sparkling Linoleum tiles.

- ▪ A bubbling metal indoor water feature.

consider this type of home. Often they are people who work in a noisy, bright, and hectic environment and who want to escape to a quiet still sanctuary at night. If metal is not your element you will find an entire metal space stark and sterile. But you may still find it helpful to introduce metal into your home for specific purposes and in order to attract some metal qualities into your life.

It is not necessary to have lots of metal furniture to suggest the metal element, and you need not forsake comfort either. In order to make the most of the metal element you need to ensure your home is tidy and well organized. While a room need not have the minimal look, it shouldn't be filled with clutter. Choose one or two special objects and display these well. The sense of stillness and focus which metal provides makes it an ideal element to introduce into a study or work room. If your work involves analysis, logic, or language skills, metal is ideal to promote these left-brain activities. Metal helps us gather and process information without distraction from our senses. It is very much a mental element which helps us to detach from our emotions and see things more clearly. Use metal furniture and fittings to create a clean, orderly, and tidy room but remember that too much metal may dampen your initiative and creativity. If you are involved in other types of business, it will be sufficient to introduce metal in smaller items. Get a metal wastebasket, letter tray, and pen tidy. This will help bring order to your office without interfering with your other abilities.

Even if you don't work from home, metal can be an asset. Everyone has to deal with household bills and correspondence and metal has a natural affinity with money and financial matters. Place a single metal object on the table, as a mark of intention, which will focus your mind on getting the task done quickly and efficiently. The metal element is also ideal to incorporate into a garage

or shed. It will help you keep it tidy and use the space most efficiently.

Although the metal element is closely associated with the logical mind, it can also help you to keep your body in shape. The focusing and calming qualities of metal in a home gym will help you integrate the mind and body. Working out in such a space will allow your mind to control your body in a safe and structured way, so that you build up your physical strength in a systematic program.

Metal objects are smooth and cool, and a room full of metal energy is light and airy. These qualities are all conducive to both physical action and relaxation. In addition you can add the soothing and cooling sounds of water.

There is a trend toward using more metal in the kitchen, which is favored by those who live in modern loft-style apartments. Metal will help you maintain a well-organized and clean kitchen, and help you to prepare and serve food efficiently. This is why metal is a popular material for canteen and restaurant kitchens, but you have to decide whether this is the attitude to food you wish to cultivate. In the dining room, too, metal will reinforce the idea that food is a means of servicing your body, and something you should do in the shortest time with the least distraction.

In the bedroom the metal element can promote good deep sleep. A metal bed will tap in to the unconscious mind allowing it to relax and unwind during the night. On the other hand too much metal will not be emotionally supportive and too much metal coldness in the bedroom will not stimulate sensuality or benefit your sex life.

Metal works well with water, so a bathroom which includes some metal energy is an asset. It may be that you want to have some metal bathroom accessories, or you could create a cool and refreshing bathroom by just using pale tiles, large mirrors, and white towels

Introducing the metal element into your home will help with the following:

■ Organizing your life better.

■ When you have to make plans or attend to financial matters.

■ Communicating more directly and effectively.

■ Focusing and concentrating on one thing at a time.

THE SHINY SURFACE OF THIS TABLE REFLECTS THE
QUALITIES OF THE METAL OBJECTS PLACED ON IT. THE
METAL ELEMENT ENCOMPASSES SHARPNESS, DEFINITION,
AND PURITY OF FORM AND FUNCTION.

Color

To convey metal energy, color is kept to a minimum in order not to detract from the bold lines and singular purpose of the material itself. Although metal is linked to the cold winter season and the color white, a metal interior doesn't have to be clinical and sterile. Like all colors there are many different shades of white in nature. You only have to look around you on a winter's day to see how snow and ice reflect the shorter wavelengths and thus appear a startling blue-white. If you look closely at a white pebble or rock you will see that it probably has tinges of gray, blue, or violet in it and many white flowers are really a soft creamy color. All these tones of white blend well together and you can use them in a room to enforce the integrating power of metal.

Although we usually associate metal with a minimal interior, you can also create a comfortable and peaceful space by combining several shades of white together with interesting textures. A variety of whites will have the effect of brightening your home, especially in winter when the days are shorter or in early spring when you feel your home needs freshening up. If you don't want to live in an all-white room, you could also choose from a variety of delicate shades of silver, gray, lilac, and blue. These colors embody the more reflective side of your nature, and can help bring about a quiet meditative state of mind.

Winter is also a time of strong contrasts, and the metal element can be interpreted with the dramatic use of black and white and gray. This strong color scheme will appeal to people with a definite metal character but, for many, it may be too extreme. If you find yourself in such an interior, adding pale lilac and blue silk cushions or a blue rug would improve the room's emotional support.

THERE IS A POWERFUL METAL PRESENCE IN THIS ROOM. THE ALL-WHITE INTERIOR MAKES YOU FEEL THAT YOU ARE ALMOST ENTERING A SACRED SPACE AND THE ORDERLY ARRANGEMENT OF OBJECTS CREATES A SENSE OF RITUAL.

Here are some ways you can introduce the metal element using the color white.

■ Have white loose covers made for your furniture from cotton, linen, or flax.

■ Drape a white chenille throw over a chair or coffee table.

■ Remove dark rugs and runners and replace them with pale cotton or wool dhurries.

■ Change your bed linen for crisp white bedding.

■ Use super soft white towels in the bathroom.

■ Make a display of white or cream crackle-glazed china (it need not match).

■ Lime-wash wooden side tables or kitchen units.

How the metal element affects our emotions

In traditional Chinese medicine, each element is linked to a particular emotion which, if not expressed fully, can cause imbalances within our body. Metal is associated with grief and feelings of sadness, melancholy, and disappointment. Often these feelings are accentuated in the autumn which is a time when our energy takes a downturn and, like nature, we become more self-reflective. Metal is linked to the more hidden side of our nature, so unlike the more externalized elements of fire, earth, and wood, an imbalance in the metal element is more difficult to detect. If the metal element is not in harmony, you may feel cynical, bored, and apathetic.

In common with many other cultures, the Chinese associate heavenly energies with those of the male, while female energies are linked to the earth. As metal is closely linked to the earth it holds yin energy. If there is a bias toward one or other polarities, it can create imbalances in the psyche. For example, if your relationship with your father or father figure has been problematic this often results in the metal element in the home becoming imbalanced. This can reveal itself in either a love of metal furniture and objects or alternatively you may avoid metal altogether depending on the nature of your relationship. The water element can balance the metal element by encouraging the outward flow of emotions which will assist you in resolving your feelings towards this person.

Although metal objects feel cold, this belies the fact that immense fire energy has to be applied in order to process and fashion it into a useable material. In the cycle of the five elements, it is fire which destroys metal and so can be used to control it. Cooling water helps metal solidify and take form, thus water enhances the qualities of metal. As mineral deposits were conceived within the earth, it also follows that these two elements are in harmony with one another.

Adjusting the metal element

Before adjusting the metal element, you need to assess whether you have too much or too little in your home. If you have any room with several large metal objects or furniture made from metal and you are experiencing one of the problems associated with metal imbalance, then you need to increase the fire element. (In the destructive cycle, fire controls metal.)

You can instigate an immediate change in energy by lighting a red candle or burning a joss stick and walking around the room, taking the fire element into every area. Longer-term solutions include introducing warm colors through the use of cushions, paintings, and decorative objects as well as softer and warm furnishing materials.

When the metal element is strong and in harmony in the home, it enriches your life, giving you direction and purpose. Its quality of hidden depths brings peace and quietness, and allows you time for inner reflection. It also helps you to develop the ability to see things with detachment and clarity, giving you a better perspective on life. Metal can therefore help you to create an uncluttered lifestyle and provide more focused living.

In this fast-moving and complex world, the qualities of the metal element are once again coming to the fore. Although metal is heavy, it has a welcome simplicity. It also conveys a sense of direction and purpose in its lines. All this can help us to relax the mind.

The metal home in feng shui

In feng shui, each element is linked to a season and a compass direction and in the case of metal it is linked with winter and the north. Metal is cold and devoid of bright color, so this mimics very well the season of winter and the colder weather which comes from the north.

If your house faces north, the rooms are likely to be dark and colder than houses which face the south or west. In China marriage and intimate relationships are meant to be quiet and sustaining and so a north-facing house was linked to these areas of life. The strong metal element in these homes is nurturing, not of the body, but of the emotions. If you neglect the north area of your home, metal energy will stagnate and become cold and critical. It will promote a negative attitude where you might dwell on past mistakes and become critical of yourself and others. To stimulate this area of your home, you need to balance the metal energy by introducing the controlling fire element.

A northwest-facing home is known as *chin ts'ai* and relates to your friends and new beginnings. Here the metal and water energy combine to influence your feelings and emotions toward people outside the home. You need to fill this area with sound to keep the energy moving. The sound should be clear and bright and could be made by brass instruments, panpipes, recorders, or flutes.

HERE THE PRESENCE OF THE METAL ELEMENT IS TYPIFIED NOT ONLY BY THE USE OF METAL ITSELF, BUT ALSO IN THE SYMMETRICAL AND ORDERLY ARRANGEMENT OF THE WINE BOTTLES IN THE RACK. THIS WOULD BE THE PERFECT PLACE TO PREPARE A JAPANESE-STYLE MEAL.

WATER

WATER

Physical attributes: flexibility and fluidity, regeneration, retention
Mental attributes: creative expression, imagination, perception, retention,
reflection, healing the emotions, feminine aspect
Compass direction: north
Home power center: bathroom, bedroom, and swimming pool

Here are different ways of introducing water and its qualities into the home:

■ A fish tank with swaying seaweed and blue or black fish will help you connect to your deep inner feelings, bringing these to the surface.

■ An indoor fountain, or one in a garden pond, will bring the sparkling and cleansing properties of water into your life. Fountains help us wash away the old and symbolize fresh new beginnings.

■ Water symbolism can be reflected in mirrors and glass. Make an etched glass coffee table with waves of plain and obscure swirls to convey areas of still and moving water, like ocean waves.

The spirit of water

Water has long been used for purification rights in many different religions and spiritual practices. In different cosmologies, water is the source of life. It was at sacred wells and springs that many rituals took place as water symbolized fertility and was linked to the feminine principle. Water provides a bridge between the solid world of matter and the invisible spiritual world of ether. This made its use for cleansing in spiritual practices common to cultures all over the world.

Water is all around us, in the oceans, lakes, and ice caps, as well as in the air, and these different types of water have different energies. Still water is soothing and calming, and its reflective qualities mirror the world around it. Likewise, the water element within us allows us to look deep inside ourselves so that we can allow hidden feelings and desires to come to the surface.

Moving water is much more dynamic; without flowing water, the earth would be barren and dry. We too are dependent on the movement of water in our bodies for good health. Water is not only the carrier of physical nutrition but also of emotional energy. The ability of water to "move" us has led to there being many systems of medicine that consider water to be a great healing agent. Because moving water is vibrant and alive, it is easy to understand why so many societies worshipped the spirits of water which they thought conveyed its healing properties.

Our ability as humans to emote is very important to our spiritual development and we have intuitively recognized this in much of our everyday language.

We often use the water theme to convey our feelings, as sayings like "waters of compassion" or "flood of emotions" demonstrate so well. Flowing water has a cleansing and purifying effect on our bodies and minds, and the feeling of liberation this brings helps us to express emotions and creativity.

If the water element is too strong within our body and home, we may display malleability, another trait of water. Water takes on the form of the container in which it finds itself, and in this way mirrors someone who bends their true personality in order to please others. People who are too dependent on others and who find it difficult to stand up for themselves need to connect to the strengthening characteristics of the wood element.

The reflective quality of water carries with it a watchfulness and curiosity. Its stillness encourages us to be careful, thrifty, and modest. Its depth conveys the sense of introspection and objectivity which allows us to communicate with utmost lucidity. On the other hand, moving water invites us to be imaginative and expressive. It is able to find a course through the countryside because it is curious and inventive. Moving water can therefore help promote an interest and ingenuity in our approach to solving problems in our lives.

The water interior

The water home is primarily a place that wants to be lived in. It is a simple and natural place to be, and will be filled with objects and furniture which are cherished and loved. You are likely to find a mixture of decorative styles in the water home. Furniture in this home is soft, rounded, and comfortable. Country styles are likely to predominate. These could be soft floral chintzes, linens, frilled and draped curtains, or the decor could be French style with painted furniture, tapestry, and pretty printed fabrics and soft woolen throws. Even when dark and rich colors are used, these are muted and teamed up with soft pastels.

The objects filling a water home are likely to be an eclectic mix linked to your special memories and hobbies. Family photos and mementoes will take pride of place over an objet d'art or a trendy display. The comfort of children and animals will always be important in the water home and you should not be surprised to find a dog's basket or child's toy box in the living room. For this reason the water environment truly reflects the needs and the psyche of the people living there.

Water nourishes living things, and so water features and plants play an important role in the water environment. A water home thrives where there is a pond or fountain, which may be inside or outdoors. A still pool will enhance the peace and serenity of the home, while moving water will bring out its playful and creative aspects. An aquarium with drifting seaweed and blue or black fish will keep the water element flowing in a room, while petals floating in a bowl of water will encourage love and emotional harmony.

Water has many dimensions. On the one hand it can be cool and silent, but on the other it has a very vocal voice. It can talk and chatter, whisper and roar. Many great composers have been inspired by the sounds of water. Play Handel's *Water Music*, or a tape or CD of natural water sounds to experience this quality.

The sound of a babbling brook can be created with an indoor pebble fountain. (If you change the shapes and sizes of the pebbles, you will vary the sound.) Waves breaking on a shore connect to our own inner body rhythms, helping regulate our body clocks and balancing our mood swings. The sound of a heartbeat is also connected to our inner pulse, bringing a feeling of security and warmth that we experienced in the womb. It is in a water environment that we are able to reflect on who we really are. The water element allows us to consolidate and regenerate, and makes a perfect environment in which we can relax and be ourselves without outside pressures.

Water and wood

In the creative cycle, water feeds wood, thus making plants the perfect complement to the water home. All plants need water to survive, but some plants attract the water element more than others. Water-loving plants go hand in hand with a pond or pool. Pond plants can even be grown on a patio or indoors; try growing a single waterlily in a wooden barrel or galvanized bucket. Many shade-loving plants thrive in water too. For example, ferns can create the soft coolness found around a woodland stream. The more dynamic aspects of water can be enhanced by introducing tropical plants. In a light and warm environment, palm trees make beautiful indoor plants as do many types of cacti and succulents.

WATER RESTRAINS THE EARTH ELEMENT. A RICH TAPESTRY OF TUMBLING PLANTS IN THE BACK YARD CAN MIMIC AN UNDERWATER SCENE, MAKING IT A PERFECT PLACE TO SIT QUIETLY, DAYDREAM, AND CONTEMPLATE LIFE.

It is possible to introduce the water element to your home through light:

■ Use a bubbling lava lamp which sends hundreds of bubbles up through colored liquid.

■ If you have a timber floor or are able to get access under your floor, cut a circle into it and install a reinforced glass panel. If this is lit from below, it will throw a soft moonlike glow into your room. Make sure the lighting is installed by a qualified electrician.

Enhancing the water element in the home

If you ask anyone to consider the use of water in the home, most people think of sinks, pipes, and taps, but water can be so much more than washing and plumbing. Like the other four natural elements, water has many special qualities which can enhance different areas of the home and help to attract similar qualities in ourselves.

By nature water is a material which shows amazing flexibility and fluidity, changing its shape and dimensions to suit the space in which it is contained. Its continuous movement suggests a flow of energy which reflects in us an ability to adapt to and bring out the best qualities of our home environment. Water has transformative qualities too, for it can change itself from a visible tangible form into an ethereal, invisible one. So the water element can help you to express your inner thoughts and feelings, bringing the unconscious to the conscious.

One of the most appealing things about water is its reflective qualities, which is why it has always been an element closely associated with the moon. The moon governs the water element in all living things, and the tides and forces within the earth and our body rhythms are strongly related to the waxing and waning of the moon. Symbolically the moon is linked to the feminine principle and its reflective qualities mirror our own need for self-reflection.

As we continue to pursue a more indoor lifestyle we are losing our connection with natural cycles and rhythms. This greatly contributes to us losing our sense of direction and purpose in life. The more we dissociate ourselves from nature, the less able we are to care for our own well-being, for

THE MOON GOVERNS THE WATER ELEMENT AND ALSO OUR ABILITY FOR SELF-REFLECTION. THIS DRAMATIC POOL WILL REFLECT THE CHANGING PATTERNS OF THE SKY WHILE ALSO HELPING TO REVEAL THE INNER FEELINGS AND DESIRES OF THOSE WHO BATHE IN IT.

nature provides everything we need to keep us in perfect health. By introducing the water element into our homes we can reestablish the connection with the softer, more nurturing, and supportive side of our nature.

Feminine energy is not exclusive to women but rather symbolizes feminine attributes of love, intuition, protection, cooperation, and tolerance. These characteristics are very closely associated with our unconscious mind, making the water element particularly active while we sleep. As the water element works through the subtle levels of your psyche, it can open your receptivity to creativity and love thus making it the perfect element to introduce into your bedroom.

As most people tend to close windows against cold at night, it is better to bring the water element into the bedroom symbolically rather than using the real thing, which might create a damp atmosphere. To enhance the water element in a bedroom, use fine lightweight fabrics like muslin for curtains and bed-drapes, and luxuriate in some soft shiny satin sheets. Paint pale pastels and thin washes or glazes on the walls using colors found in abalone and mother-of-pearl shells. This will give your bedroom a dream-like quality.

Silver is the metal closely associated with the moon and water, and so is in total harmony with the water element. Silver-framed photographs in the bedroom and natural objects like white shells or mosaics of mirror pieces can enhance the water theme. Glass has the same reflective qualities as water, so find some glass bedside tables or perhaps a glass-topped dressing table over which you could hang a decorative round mirror.

Like the moon, the water element is enhanced by soft reflected light which creates a flattering and

THE WATER ELEMENT HELPS US LINK TO OUR INTUITION AND ENJOY A SENSE OF MYSTERY. IN THIS DREAMY BEDROOM THE BLUE WALLS AND SOFTLY DRAPED CURTAINS CREATE A RELAXING PLACE WHERE WE CAN LOOK TO OUR IMAGINATIVE AND CREATIVE SPIRIT.

romantic atmosphere. Uplighters with etched glass shades lift our vision upward and create a soft moonlight effect.

A good time to introduce the water element into your home is if you ever feel you are in a rut, suffering from mental exhaustion, or needing a more creative and intuitive approach to life. Water allows you time to think and reflect, helping you to relax so you become more flexible and feel more able to "go with the flow."

The water element in the home

You can use the water element in the living room to create a visionary and sacred space. This is especially in tune with water personalities. In this room they can relax and explore their intuitive nature. As in the bedroom, a living space filled with water energy works through the emotions so you can create a home with a sympathetic and caring atmosphere. This will be a room where you can share your innermost thoughts or, if you are spiritually inclined, it will be a place of mystery and contemplation.

The cool and quiet atmosphere provided by the water element may not be so suitable for some dining areas, as the color blue has been found to suppress the appetite and can be depressing. On the other hand, a moving water feature can enliven a dining area and promote sharing, while in the kitchen water will contribute to a feeling of well-being especially when combined with the nourishing vibrations of wood.

Our physical bodies are made up of around 70 percent water which is one of the basic requirements for maintaining life. You should always make sure that you drink the best quality water that you can obtain. Chemicals and other toxic pollutants can enter the water supply so it is well worth investing in a good water filter. This can be attached directly to your incoming water supply or you can buy a filtering jug. Both these methods of purifying water are much more economical than buying bottled water.

Ways to enhance the water element in your home:

■ Introduce a small indoor fountain allowing the water to dance on shells rather than pebbles.

■ Create soft lighting using silver-colored lamps with twinkling beaded shades.

■ Use moiré and water-mark silks and satin fabrics.

■ Play a tape of ocean waves or a babbling brook.

■ Make a collection and display of pearly glassware or silver.

■ Paint walls in a pale lilac or light pearl gray.

■ Use strong blues, greens, and purples as accent colors on doors, window frames, dadoes or picture rails, or in accessories such as rugs, cushions, and pictures.

■ Choose patterns that incorporate horizontal wavy lines and swirling shapes.

■ Paint floors with glossy white paint.

■ Install a round window high in the wall to view the moon and sky.

The water home in feng shui

Water in feng shui is linked to abundance. This refers not only to physical wealth but also spiritual wealth. In the landscape, the presence of water is extremely auspicious as rivers are considered to be the dragon's veins through which Chi energy flows.

A house which is located next to or nearby water is usually a place where the residents will thrive, especially if the house faces the water. Ideally all houses should face a river, a sea, or a pond. The quality of the water is also important, and the movement of the water will indicate whether the Chi is stagnant or moving too quickly. The direction of the flow will also indicate whether good fortune is flowing to or away from the house. You can use water to attract prosperity by introducing it into your home. Traditionally an aquarium or fish symbol was placed in the east of the home to attract wealth.

The north side of your home is connected to the water element, and in feng shui this is the area which is linked to relationships and marriage. The Chi in this area is quiet, nurturing, and sustaining. It helps to envelop you in love, comfort, and warmth. The northeast side of your home is related to children and family. This is the area of thunder which arouses and stimulates the formation of water and therefore promotes strong relationships with your children and family. While the north and east directions relate to your relationships within the family, the northwest promotes loyal and harmonious attachments with your friends. You can use the water element to stimulate one or more of these areas of your life by introducing water or water symbolism into the corresponding areas of your home.

The ideal water home should face south. Then it will convey the warmth and love afforded by the sun (that warms the water element within us) and spread loving vibrations throughout the home.

WATER NOURISHES THE WOOD ELEMENT. IN THIS BATHROOM THESE TWO NATURAL ELEMENTS WORK EXTREMELY WELL TOGETHER TO MAKE BATHING A PLAYFUL AND JOYFUL EXPERIENCE. THE TREASURED COLLECTION OF SHELLS ALSO CONJURES UP MEMORIES OF HAPPY TIMES SPENT BESIDE THE SEA.

Add the following essential oils to pure water to cleanse your home:

■ For electronic smog and chemical pollutants, use lavender, tea tree, and pine needle.

■ For illness, use tea tree, lavender, and clove.

■ For nervous tension and anxiety, use neroli, sandalwood, and sweet orange.

■ For depressive thoughts and anger use palmarosa, geranium, and chamomile.

Water rituals for the home

Our homes harbor a wealth of different pollutants which are toxic to body and mind. These may be the result of chemical vapors and fumes given off by many building materials and household products, or they may have more subtle causes. Our brains generate energy in the form of thought waves. These waves create vibrations which spread out around us like ripples in a pond. The energy created permeates the furnishings and can even enter and be held within the fabric of the building itself. Positive thoughts can instill your home with a sense of happiness and harmony while anger and negative thoughts will create an unhappy and unhealthy atmosphere. Water has always been known for its purifying and cleansing qualities and you can use it very simply and effectively to clear out any physical or emotional smog from your home.

Purifying your home with a spray

Spray misting is a simple and quick way to spring clean and detoxify your home using aroma. By using different scents, you will be able to rid your home of different types of negative vibration.

You will need a plastic or glass bottle with a pump-action spray. I use a plant spray which you can buy at most garden shops. Fill the bottle with warm water (about 4 tablespoons) which helps disperse the oils. Add to this a combination of 15 drops of essential oil or a combination of oils. Walk around the room and spray cleansing mist in the corners and then into the middle.

A water ritual to attract wealth and abundance

Water is the source of life. It nourishes the earth and plant life, and it also nourishes the human spirit. This connection with growth and renewal makes water the best element to use in order to attract natural abundance into your life. Change and growth only comes with movement, and in order to allow positive energy into your home, you need moving water.

Place some pure water, or if you can get it, water from a holy well or spring, into a large flat glass bowl. Put the bowl of water on a coffee table, and with the index finger of your right hand, move the water in a counterclockwise direction so that you create a spiral. Then with the index finger of your left hand, create a spiral of water in the other direction. Using your right hand again, trace a figure eight in the water. Change hands and do the same with your left hand.

By spiraling the water in this way you will be energizing it, bringing together the masculine and feminine principles in a creative force field of energy. Natural abundance and wealth are generated from this union and so this simple ritual will encourage them into your life.

THIS SIMPLE DISPLAY OF SHELLS AND A WHITE-COLORED STARFISH EFFECTIVELY BRINGS THE WATER ELEMENT INSIDE THE HOME TO REMIND US OF THE MYSTERY OF LIFE. IT IS THROUGH THE WATER ELEMENT THAT WE CAN EXPRESS OUR DESIRE FOR HONESTY AND TRUTH.

HONORING THE FIVE ELEMENTS

HARMONIZING THE FIVE ELEMENTS IN YOUR HOME

Living in a house which is in harmony with your basic elemental nature will enhance your feeling of well-being, but there should also be a place in your home in which you honor all five elements.

This can be achieved in three ways. Firstly you can create a symbolic representation of each of the five elements and place these together to create a shrine. A shrine should not be viewed as some pagan or New Age symbol, but as a reflection of your inner being which will help you focus on the different aspects in your life in a more balanced way. Secondly, you can harmonize the five elements in your main living area by intuitively aligning and manipulating the furniture and furnishings. Thirdly, you can introduce single elements into your five main rooms, so that together these create elemental harmony throughout the house.

As our lives are constantly changing and we experience different moods and feelings, it would be difficult to adjust all the elements in your home continually and in a totally literal way. If we tried this, we would constantly be changing and rearranging furniture and furnishings. Instead it is easier to use a symbolic representation of the five elements to invoke a sense of harmony and balance.

Most people have a natural love of collecting and decorating. This is not something we do haphazardly, but in a meaningful and aesthetic way. This gives us immense satisfaction and is a means of bringing spirituality into everyday life, for caring for our home is the same as caring for our soul. These symbolic qualities represent the circle of life on which we can trace the cycle of our own lives. Achieving harmony of the natural elements externally will be automatically reflected internally, creating a feeling of wholeness and connection between all the different parts of our being.

The earth gives rise to all life and represents birth, while the wood element represents childhood and energetic growth. The fire element reflects youthful and creative energy, while water connects to maturity and a more reflective time of our life. Metal links to old age and death. Every stage is equal to each other and is an essential part of life through which we all must pass. Bringing this natural flow to our attention is a good way to help us pass gracefully from one stage to another, while respecting those who are going through a different stage.

Honoring the five elements in a shrine

We can honor all life by introducing the five elements into our homes. One special way of doing this is by creating a shrine which contains objects reflecting each of the five elements.

To start with, walk around your home and collect a dozen or so objects which have a special significance to you. These may include such things as a piece of family jewelry, a feather or stone that you have picked up on a walk, or a much-loved book. Put these objects together in front of you and assign a different element to each of them. You do not have to allocate the elements in a literal way. For example, a book, although made from paper (the wood element), may be a story set at the seaside and therefore carries strong water energy for you.

When you have linked each object to an element, count up the number of items related to each. Do you have more fire, water, earth, metal, or wood objects? Several objects of the same element will reveal how you view the world. The objects will also tell a story about your own cycle of life. Place the objects in a row, starting with the one you have had the longest and finishing with your newest acquisition. You will then be able to link different times of your life and experiences to the different elements. If you had a bad association with any of the elements, it is a good idea to try to integrate this element back into your life. If any of the five elements is missing, this will tell you that you need to focus more time and attention on the corresponding part of your life.

If the fire element is not there, you are likely to be missing out on the enjoyment of the here and now. Perhaps you need to be more spontaneous and allow your inner creativity to find expression. Should the water element be missing, you need to resolve issues relating to past emotions. By finding an object related to water, you will be taking a positive step towards externalizing your inner feelings.

If the wood element is missing in your collection, you may be stuck in a rut and should reflect on ways you could nourish some inner growth. The metal element is often linked to air and the mind, and it may be that you are reacting too emotionally to situations, rather than exercising mental discretion and detachment. In this case, the metal element will empower you to become more balanced in your outlook, without being cold and calculating.

Lastly, should you find that you have no earth object, this will tell you that you need to slow down and focus on the more practical and perhaps mundane things in life. Without earth, we become wanderers and dreamers, with little sense of belonging or purpose. Reestablishing your earth connection can help you bring your ideas and dreams into reality. Often you find that highly creative people are also naturally drawn to gardening or pottery. Taking up an activity which connects you to the earth is the perfect foil if your life involves a high degree of mental work, whether analytical or creative. This is because you can lose touch with reality and become lost in a world of

your own. Even if you don't go in for hobbies, merely touching and arranging pebbles or ceramic pots in your home will bring you down to earth.

Once you have completed the previous task, now select one object to represent each of the five elements. If you are missing any element, look for something else to include to complete your collection. By introducing a symbolic representation of each element you will invoke a sense of balance and harmony in your life.

The earth element can be embodied in an obvious way with rocks, pebbles, and stones or by an earthenware pot or stone sculpture. Water is always present in the home by way of the plumbing system, but we also need to pay our respects mindfully to this element. Bring the sacred essence of water to your attention through a glass object or by placing some water in a beautiful container. Fire can be honored with a candle, lantern, or light. The intensity of the flame can be reinforced by placing a mirror behind it. You can also invoke the spirit of fire by lighting a joss stick, or burning essential oils or incense. Hang colored pieces of glass so that they not only catch the light, but also tinkle in the breeze. Choose a clear quartz crystal, moonstone or other white-colored stone. Wood can be reflected by a single flower, plant, woven or paper object.

If we consider the air element as carrying the breath of life or Chi, we can use it as a way of instilling energy into the other elements. Air can act as a light switch, turning on power. The air element can be conjured up in many ways. A fluttering feather or colorful ribbons, strings of beads and tiny bells. If you have created your shrine in an enclosed space, by consciously imagining that you are breathing white light into your objects you can introduce the air element to the shrine yourself.

Your eye and your heart will soon tell you whether you have selected the right objects. Sometimes a piece just doesn't feel right, and it seems to spoil the balance and radiance of the other objects around it. Many times you find that you need to replace one or more of your treasures over a period of time, when you get the feeling that it has lost its power and sparkle. In reality you will be creating a shrine to honor and celebrate life and the passage of time. You will also need to decide where you would like to make your shrine. You could display it on a mantelpiece, display shelf, or on a coffee table. Alternatively you may decide to make your shrine a secluded place and keep your objects out of sight. In order to make a private collection you could set out your objects in a cupboard, drawer, or even in a shoe box which you can decorate.

Spend time tending your shrine as you would a garden, for its care will mirror your attitude toward yourself. We are naturally attracted to some elements more than others, and this will give you an idea about your inner balance. So as you look after your shrine over a period of time, moving and arranging the objects, you will learn much about yourself. As your connection with the spiritual flow increases, you will befriend those aspects of yourself with which you once felt less at ease.

THE RICHNESS AND WARMTH OF THE EARTH AND WOOD
ELEMENTS IMMEDIATELY CREATE A WELCOMING
ATMOSPHERE IN THIS HALLWAY. THE REFLECTIVE GLASS
BOTTLES ADD A TOUCH OF BOTH THE FIRE AND THE WATER
ELEMENTS WHICH RESULTS IN A WONDERFULLY BALANCED
SPACE WHERE THESE FOUR ELEMENTS ARE IN HARMONY.

Balancing all the elements

Once you feel confident about balancing the physical elements in your home, you could ensure that all five elements are present in your main living area. The harmonious balance between these can only be achieved through your own observation and sensitivity. A good way to check this is by sitting in meditation in the room and by allowing the spirit of the elements to talk to you directly. Often you will sense that there is too much or too little of a particular element. Sometimes you feel that one object or item of furniture is too powerful and is draining the energy in the room. If this happens you could remove it, but it may well have the same effect elsewhere in the house. A better solution is to use your knowledge of the controlling cycle of the elements to increase the element which will minimize its destabilizing effect.

How the elements affect our moods

Another way of assessing the energy in a room is by your physical, emotional, and mental responses while you are in that room. A strong presence of one of the elements is bound to affect your moods in an adverse way.

Fire is linked to our creative energy, but also our determination to succeed. Fire also has strong associations with anger and the color red, and this type of anger is born out of frustration and a feeling that our path is blocked. If fire energy is out of control in our homes, we are likely to become irritable and impatient, and may ignite family arguments. This will ultimately affect your other personal and work relationships because you can easily lose your sense of reality and direction. When you have been in a "fire" place you need to be grounded, which will help you to turn your ideas into reality and help them take form.

If there is too much earth energy in a room, it

IN THE CREATIVE CYCLE FIRE CREATES EARTH, WHICH IN TURN CREATES METAL. HERE THESE POWERFUL ELEMENTS WORK IN HARMONY, EACH SUPPORTING THE NEXT.

will make you feel sleepy and lethargic. In homes with a dominant earth energy you often find people slumped in front of the TV. You need to adjust the earth energy when you feel stuck in a rut and unable to change or improve your situation.

It is seldom that a living room has too much water energy, although a room with large areas of glass and highly reflective materials will encourage daydreaming and a sleepy, impractical outlook on life. Water rooms are best kept to bedrooms where these qualities are an asset. In rooms where the metal element is too powerful, the occupants are likely to be introverted and prone to routine and orderliness. A metal room is not a place you can feel relaxed and sociable, and often it has a cold and formal atmosphere.

If the wood element is too strong, it can have far-reaching effects. On one occasion, I was called in to harmonize the energy in a home belonging to a couple who were having difficulties in their marriage. It turned out that all their arguments started in the kitchen. It would be natural to suppose that the fire element was too strong, but in this room the wood element was running riot. Large heavy beams and dark timber kitchen units dominated the room and so it was not surprising that the problems the couple were experiencing involved feelings of jealousy and lack of trust. Both these emotions are linked to wood. As both of them disliked the kitchen, inherited from the previous owner, they decided to redecorate. The heavy wooden beams were painted white, the color related to the controlling element of metal. Although the new units were also timber, these were much lighter in color and had stainless steel handles. Almost immediately, the kitchen became a much more pleasurable place to be and the arguments were replaced by happier evenings.

While I am not suggesting that the kitchen was the underlying root of their marital problems, the supportive environment that the kitchen provided after the elements were harmonized definitely created a more relaxed and calmer atmosphere.

When one particular object is too forceful, you can reduce its dominance by adding another element to balance its effect:

- When EARTH is dominant, add something that represents the wood element into the room.

- When WOOD is dominant, add something that represents the metal element into the room.

- When METAL is dominant, add something that represents the fire element into the room.

- When FIRE is dominant, add something that represents the water element into the room.

- When WATER is dominant, add something that represents the earth element into the room.

Harmonizing the elements in the whole house, room by room

Getting a balance of all five elements in your home should not be approached like a mathematical problem. Rather than looking for and adhering to exacting rules, it is better to take a more open and intuitive approach. As long as all the elements are present, even in different rooms, you will enjoy a happy and harmonious home.

While it is a good idea to honor all five elements together somewhere in your home, most rooms have a natural sympathy with one of the elements. It is easy to harness this natural tendency and accentuate these elements by placing an object of the appropriate element in that room. If you want to be more adventurous you could create a more permanent connection by decorating the room in a style and colors which reflect the sympathetic element.

By intentionally linking the rooms in your home to the five elements, you will achieve overall harmony, while enjoying an inspirational and interesting interior.

Most modern homes are made up of the living room, kitchen and dining area, bedroom, bathroom, and study. You may have another room such as a music or hobby room rather than a study, and this can be counted as your fifth space.

The living room is the place which expresses your personality and lifestyle. It also often houses a fireplace, so this is the best room to carry the fire element. The nature of fire is that of continual movement and change, and like life is full of surprises. Its energy is very linked to the present. It is in the living areas that we can be the most creative and indulge our whims. Change this room around to suit your moods or in relation to the seasons. Add decorative objects and furnishings for different occasions and enjoy this flexible and inspirational space.

The kitchen and dining room are very much to do with nurturing and growth, so these areas have a natural connection with the wood element. Your elemental connection need not be a permanent one, but a ritual which you can perform as and when you like. Special seasonal and festive meals have been an age-old way of honoring the plant kingdom and the wood element. Make a colorful salad of spring greens and vegetables or a Chinese feast with bamboo shoots and beansprouts. Before you eat these tantalizing delights, say a prayer or dedication to the element of wood for sharing its natural abundance with you.

The bedroom provides a very protective and sacred place, and one which is related to the feminine principle. So the bedroom is the space to dedicate to Mother Earth. When you do this it will become a place where you can feel secure and relaxed. It will also encourage a sense of bodily ease and be a place where you can express your sexuality. You can tune in to the nurturing qualities of the earth by making your bedroom a sensual and tactile part of your home. Fill it with beautiful aromas, textures, and sound. It is the perfect place to walk barefoot or to relax on colorful cushions on the floor.

THIS BLAZING COAL FIRE KEEPS THE DOMINANT METAL ELEMENT IN CHECK. THE ELEMENT OF FIRE ALWAYS BRINGS MOVEMENT AND ENERGY TO A ROOM, MAKING IT A MORE COMFORTABLE PLACE IN WHICH TO SOCIALIZE AND COMMUNICATE WITH OTHERS.

The bathroom is the sacred place of water, and this element of fluidity can be amplified by focusing on our emotions. Tune in to your inner feelings and desires when you are lying in a warm bath or taking a shower. Wash away your stress and worries by sprinkling water over your head and face using a specially chosen container. Choose one made from metal, blue glass, or even mother-of-pearl shell. While an element may already be present in the fabric and services of our homes, this is a very literal and physical manifestation of the cosmic forces. So although your bathroom has a good supply of water, this utilitarian provision has little to do with the spiritual essence of water. It is only when we do something "with intent" that we can understand the meaning behind these elemental forces. Washing is about cleansing not only the body but the mind. The water element is linked to the past, and we can use it to wash away our past associations and ties.

The home office or study is bound to be a place where you will find the metal element because so much office equipment and furniture is made from metal. The metal element is very much to do with the future and the domain of the mind, but it is only by consciously honoring the metal element in your work environment that you will really harness its organizational and integrative qualities. The study, therefore, is the best place to organize your life and make plans about your future.

Once you have honored each of the elements in any of the ways I have described, you will have created a symbolic map of life with its challenges, qualities, and natural rhythms. This natural flow of energy with its universal laws of relationships will be mirrored in your body and life. Now is the time to celebrate your connection with the five elements and reap the rewards of living in a home where all the elements are in harmony.

THE RITUAL OF DAILY LIFE CAN OFTEN LEAVE US FEELING HEAVY AND EARTHBOUND. IN THIS BATHROOM, THERE IS A HARMONY OF WATER, WOOD, METAL, AND FIRE, WHICH TOGETHER WILL CLEANSE AND REVITALIZE BOTH BODY AND MIND.

USEFUL ADDRESSES

Organizations

Feng Shui Guild
PO Box 766
Boulder, CO 80306
USA

Feng Shui Institute of America
PO Box 488
Wabasso, FL 32980
USA

Lighting Research Institute
120 Wall Street, 17th Floor
New York, NY 10005-4001
USA

Natural Food Associates
PO Box 210
Atlanta, TX 75551
USA

Solar Box Cookers International
1724 11th Street
Sacramento, CA 95814
USA

The Holistic Design Institute which was
founded and is run by the author offers
various home study courses and
workshops in the creation of healing
environments.

The Holistic Design Institute
Farfields House,
Jubilee Road,
Totnes, Devon, TQ9 5BP
UK
tel: +44 (0)1803 868 037
e-mail: hdi@eclipse.co.uk
http//: www.holisticdesign.co.uk

The Ecological Design Association
Slad Road,
Stroud,
Gloucestershire, GL5 1QW
UK

The Feng Shui Society
377 Edgware Road,
London, W2 1BT
UK

Feng Shui Network International
2 Thayer Street,
London, W1M 5LG
UK

International Association for Colour Therapy
PO Box 3,
Potters Bar,
Hertfordshire, EN6 3ET
UK

Iris International School of Colour Therapy
Farfields House,
Jubilee Road,
Totnes, Devon, TQ9 5BP
UK

Suppliers

Air Purifiers

National EnviroAlert Company
297 Lake Street
Waltham, MA 02154
USA

Purity Home Product Inc.
Box 397
Milersport, OH 43046
USA

London Ionizer Centre
65 Endell Street,
London, WC2H 9AJ
UK

Mountain Breeze
Peel House, Peel Road,
Skelmersdale, Lancashire, WN8 9PT
UK

Bamboo and wicker

Bamboo & Rattan Works Inc.
470 Oberlin Avenue
South Lakewood, NJ 08701
USA

Bielecky Brothers Inc.
305 East 61st Street
New York, NY 10021
USA

Oxfam
272 Banbury Road,
Oxford, OXC2 7DZ
UK

Full-spectrum lights

Truelite SML
Unit 4, Wye Trading Estate,
London Road, High Wycombe,
Buckinghamshire, HP11 1LH
UK

Heating

Amerec Sauna Steam
PO Box 40569
Bellevue, WA 98004
USA

Jacuzzi Whirlpool Bath
PO Drawer J
Walnut Creek, CA 94596
USA

Low-energy Supply Systems
84 Colston Street,
Bristol, BS1 5BB
UK

Natural Fabrics

Natural Fabrics
14 E. Cota Street,
Santa Barbara, CA 93101
USA

Sew Natural Fabrics by Mail
Box 428,
Middlesex, NC 27557
USA

The Crafts Council
12 Waterloo Place,
London, W1M 5LG
UK

The Sheep Shop
54 Neal Street,
London, WC2
UK

Natural Flooring

Country Floors Inc.
15 East 166th Street
New York, NY 10003
USA

JL Powell & Company Inc.
600 South Madison Street
Whiteville, NC 28472
USA

The Crucial Trading Company
77 Westbourne Park Road,
London, W2
UK

Fired Earth
Twyford Mill,
Oxford Road,
Adderbury,
Oxfordshire, OX17 3HP
UK

Three Shires
3 Ptarmigan Place,
Townsend Drive,
Attleborough Fields,
Nuneaton,
Warwickshire, CV11 6RX
UK

Natural Paints

Paint Effects
2426 Fillmore Street
San Francisco, CA 94115
USA

Crown Berger
PO Box 37,
Crown House,
Hollins Road,
Darwin,
Lancashire, BB3 0BG
UK

Farrow and Ball Ltd.
24-26 Uddens Trading Estate,
Wimborne,
Dorset, BH21 7NL
UK

New Wool Matresses

The Fairchild Co.
2a Willeton Trading Estate,
Willeton,
Taunton,
Somerset, TA4 4RF
UK

Futon Company
82-83 Tottenham Court Road,
London, W1P 9HD
UK

SAD and Light Therapy

Outside In Ltd.
Unit 21,
Scotland Road Estate,
Dry Drayton,
Cambridge, CB3 8AT
UK

Water filters

Action Filter Inc.
777 Wyoming Avenue,
Kingston, PA 18704
USA

FURTHER READING

The Healing Home – Creating the Perfect Place to Live with Color, Aroma, Light and Other Natural Elements
Suzy Chiazzari
U.K. Ebury Press, 1998
U.S. Trafalgar Square, 1998

The Complete Book of Color – Using Color for Lifestyle, Health and Well-being
Suzy Chiazzari
U.K. Element, 1999

Feng Shui for the Soul – How to Create a Harmonious Environment That Will Nurture and Sustain You
Denise Linn
U.K. Rider Books, 1999
U.S. Hay House, 1999

Sacred Space – Enhancing the Energy of Your Home and Office with Feng Shui
Denise Linn
U.K. Ebury Press, 2000
U.S. Ballantine Books, 2000

Space Clearing – How to Purify and Create Harmony in Your Home
Denise Linn
U.K. Ebury Press, 2000
U.S. Contemporary, 2000

Feng Shui for Modern Living – Bring Harmony, Health, Wealth and Happiness into Your Life
Stephen Skinner
U.S. Trafalgar Square, 2000

The Natural House Book
David Pearson
U.K. Conran Octopus
U.S. Fireside

Between Heaven and Earth – A Guide to Chinese Medicine
Harriet Beinfield and Efrem Korngold
U.S. Ballantine Wellspring, New York, 1991

The Re-enchantment of Everyday Life
Thomas Moore
U.K. Hodder and Stoughton, 1996
U.S. HarperCollins, 1996

ACKNOWLEDGMENTS

pp. 2-3 International Interiors/Paul Ryan; p. 5 Houses & Interiors/Verne; p. 7 Abode; pp. 8-9 Jake Fitzjones; p. 11 Interior Archive/Herbert Ypma; p. 15 Interior Archive/Henry Wilson; pp. 18-19 International Interiors/Paul Ryan; p. 20 Axiom/William Shaw; p. 23 Arcaid/Alan Weintraub; p. 24 International Interiors/ Paul Ryan; p. 27 Interior Archive/Simon Upton; pp. 28-29 Arcaid/Richard Waite; p. 33 Axiom/Heidi Grassley; p. 34 Arcaid/Richard Waite; pp. 36-37 Axiom/Chris Coe; p. 39 Arcaid/Farrell Green; p. 41 Interior Archive/Simon Brown; p. 45 Arcaid/Simon Kenny/Belle; p. 46 Jake Fitzjones; pp. 48-49 Axiom/Chris Coe; pp. 50-51 Houses & Interiors/Roger Brooks; pp. 54-55 International Interiors/Paul Ryan; p. 57 International Interiors/Paul Ryan; pp. 58-59 Arcaid/Alan Weintraub; pp. 60-61 Abode; pp. 62-63 Jake Fitzjones; pp. 64-65 International Interiors/Paul Ryan; pp. 68-69 Houses & Interiors/Bruce Hemming; p. 73 International Interiors/Paul Ryan; pp. 74-75 Interior Archive/Simon Upton; p. 77 Abode; p. 79 Arcaid/Richard Bryant; pp. 80-81 Houses & Interiors/Simon Butcher; pp. 82-83 Houses & Interiors/Mark Bolton; pp. 84-85 Houses & Interiors/Peter Reid; p. 87 Houses & Interiors/Steve Hawkins; pp. 88-89 Arcaid/Richard Bryant; p. 91 International Interiors/Paul Ryan; pp. 92-93 Interior Archive/Simon Upton; p. 95 Abode; pp. 96-97 International Interiors/Paul Ryan; p. 99 Abode; p. 100-101 International Interiors/Paul Ryan; p. 103 Houses & Interiors/Nick Johnson; pp. 104-105 Arcaid/Earl Carter/Belle; p. 106 Houses & Interiors/Steve Sparrow; pp. 108-109 Jake Fitzjones; p. 111 International Interiors/Paul Ryan; pp. 112-113 Interior Archive/Edina van der Wyck; pp. 116-117 Abode; p. 118 International Interiors/Paul Ryan; p. 121 Abode; p. 123 Jake Fitzjones.

INDEX

Numbers in italics refer to captions

allergy sufferers 78
aluminum 67
Aristotle 11
aromatherapy oils 86, 110
Art Deco 42
Art Nouveau 56
Arts and Crafts movement 56
Ayurvedic system 11

bamboo structures 53
bathrooms 53, *85*, 94, *109*, 122, *122*
beach cottages 44
beams, wooden 35, 119
bedrooms 53, 68, 94, 107, *107*, 120
boat houses 44
bonfires 72
bookcases and shelves 58, *58*
books 57, 58
bricks 38, 82
Buddhism 32, 72

candles 67, 71, 72, 81, 86, 98, 115
center, finding 82
central heating 66, 67
ceramics 78, 81
chanting 72
Chi (energy) 6, 10, 30, 71, 109
church architecture 42, 47-48
cold houses 30-31
colors 12
  earth 78
  fire 70
  and metal 97, 98
  and water *26*, 107
  and wood 60
copper 67, 71, 90
creation myths 76
creative cycles 12-13, 16, 44, 114, *119*
crystal pendants 71

dampness in homes 30, 31
drafty homes 30

earth 11, 76
  buildings 31, 38, *38*, 77
  and colors 12, 78, 83
  and emotions and mood 119
  environments 36, *36*
  establishing connections 82, 83, 85,
    86, 115
  and food 78
  home interiors *22*, 76-77
  personalities 17, 22
  rituals 86
  and seasons 11, 16
  and yin and yang 12
earthenware objects 78, 82
electrical equipment 71, 110
emotions and moods 17, 98, 115, 119,
  120, 122; *see also* personality types
Empedocles 11
environment *see* landscape

fabrics 56, 57, 60, 70, 107
feminine energy 107
feng shui 10, 61, 71, 78, 98-99, 109
filters, water 107
fire 11, 14, 64
  accessories 70
  buildings *21*, *47*, 47-48, *48*
  colors 12, *21*, 70, 73
  and emotions and mood 115, 119
  and feng shui 71
  home interiors 64, 66-68, 71
  in landscapes 31, 47
  and metal 40
  personalities 17, 21
  rituals 72-73
  and seasons 11, 16
  and yang 12
fireplaces 60, 66, 67, *68*, 71, *90*, 120, *120*

fire stations 47
fish tanks 102
floor coverings, natural 53
floors, wooden 52, 53, *54*, 103
flowers *see* plants and flowers
food 14, 78, 120
"fool's gold" 67
fountains 44, 102, 103, 107

Gaia theory 6, 76
gardens 43, 85, *103*
glass 14, 44, 102, 107, 115
  see also mirrors
gold 67, 90
Gothic architecture 42, 47

hallways 67, *116*
home offices 94, 122
hot homes 30, 31
houseboats 44

incense, burning 86
intention, ritual of 86
iron 67, 90
Ishvarakrsna: *Samkhya-karujas* 11

jewelry 67, 115
Jung, Carl 11

kitchens 120
  earth 76, 78
  and fire 68, 71
  and metal *92*, 94
  and wood 53, 119

lacquerware 70
lamps and lanterns 53, *54*, 60, *60*, *72*, 81,
  103
landscapes 30-31
lava lamps *103*
lead 90

lighthouses 47

lighting 66, 81, *81*, *see also* lamps

Linn, Denise: *Feng Shui for the Soul* 78

log cabins *see* wood buildings

Lovelock, James: Gaia theory 6, 76

magnetic fields 44, *44*, 85, 92

Mediterranean-style homes 77, *78*

mercury 90

metal 11, 90

  as building material 14, 40, *41*, 42

  and colors 12, *92*, 94, 97, 98

  and feng shui 98-99

  and fire element 67-68

  in home interiors *25*, *64*, 90, *90*, 92, *92*,
    94, 95, *95*, *97*, 98, *99*, *120*

  in landscapes 31, 40

  and moods and emotions 98, 119, 122

  personalities 17, 25, *25*

  and seasons 11, 16

  and water 98, 107

  and yin and yang 12

mirrors *14*, 42, *64*, 67, 71, 102

mobile homes *41*, 42

moods *see* emotions

Morris, William 56

moving house 77, 82, 85

music 72, 86, 99, 103

oils, aromatherapy 86, 110

paints: from natural pigments 78

  see also colors

paper 57

  lampshades and lanterns 53, *54*, 60, *60*

patios 38, 85

pebble arrangements 82, *82*

personality types 17

  earth 17, 22

  fire 17, 21

  metal 17, 25

  water 17, 26

  wood 17, 19

yin and yang 17

photographs 86, *86*, 103, 107

pictures 70, 71, 86, *86*

plants and flowers 54, *57*, 61, 66, 67, 70,
  71, 103, *103*; *see also* trees

Plato 11

pools 43, *44*, 103, *104*

public buildings 48

pyramid shapes 47, *48*, 71

reinforced steel joists (RSJs) 42

remembering, ritual of 86

rituals:

  earth 86

  fire 72-73

  water 110

rivers/riverside homes 30, 43, 109

roofs *21*, 44, *47*, 48

rooftop gardens 35, 36

Ruskin, John 56

Scandinavian architecture 44, 48

seaside houses 43, 109

seasons 11, 16; *see also* feng shui

Shaker-style homes 44

shared homes 26

shrines 114-116

silks 70, 107

silver 90, 107

springs, natural 43

stainless steel 67

staircases 66, 67

streams, underground 43-44

stress 6, 13, 110

stuffiness in homes 30

sunburst motifs 47, *64*

tactile stimulation 14, 16, 76

Tao/Taoism 6, 11, 12; *see also* feng shui

terracotta pots and tiles 38, 77, *77*

tiles 38, 42, 77, *77*, 78

tin 90, 92

touch, sense of 14, 16

tree houses 35, *35*

Tree of Life 52, 56

trees 32, *35*, 40, 52, 54, 61

Tudor style architecture 35, 56

volcanoes/volcanic rock 47

wall coverings and hangings 57, 60

wallpapers 56-57

water 30, 31, 43-44, 102

  and buildings 44

  and colors 12, *26*, 107

  and emotions and mood 17, 44, 115, 119

  and feng shui 109

  in home interiors 102-103, 104, 107, *110*

  and metal 98, 107

  personalities 17, 26

  rituals 110

  and seasons 11

  and wood 6-7, 103

  and yin 12

waterfalls 43

water features 44

water mills, converted 44

white, use of 97

windy positions 30

wood 52, *see also* paper; plants; trees

  buildings 32, *32*, 34, 48

  and colors 12, 60

  and emotions and mood 115, 119

  environments 30, 31, 32

  and feng shui 61

  in home interiors *19*, 52-53, 56, *57*, 67

  personalities 17, 19

  and seasons 11, 16

  and water 6-7, 103

  yang and yin 12

woodchip paper 57

yin and yang 12, 82, 85

  personalities 17